GCSE Edexcel

Chemistry

We'll be honest — getting the top grades in Edexcel GCSE Chemistry can be a challenge. There are lots of experiments and equations to learn, plus moles popping up everywhere.

Fortunately, our CGP Chemistry experts have written a bunch of exam-style questions to make sure you're prepped for the hardest questions the exams will throw at you. We've even included targeted analysis questions to test those tricky AO3 skills.

And that's not all! There are worked solutions to every question at the back of the book, so it's easy to check your answers and make sure you're on track for a great result.

Grade 8-9 Targeted
Exam Practice Workbook

Published by CGP

Editors:
Rob Hayman, Paul Jordin, Sarah Pattison

Contributors:
Angela McGill, David Paterson, Louise Watkins

With thanks to Sharon Keeley-Holden for the proofreading.

With thanks to Jan Greenway for the copyright research.

Data in Figure 1 on page 53 adapted from data from SPM.4, Panel (a) from IPCC, 2013: Summary for Policymakers. In: Climate Change 2013: The Physical Science Basis. Contribution of Working Group I to the Fifth Assessment Report of the Intergovernmental Panel on Climate Change [Stocker, T.F., D. Qin, G.-K. Plattner, M. Tignor, S.K. Allen, J. Boschung, A. Nauels, Y. Xia, V. Bex and P.M. Midgley (eds.)]. Cambridge University Press, Cambridge, United Kingdom and New York, NY, USA.

Graph to show trend in atmospheric CO_2 concentration and global temperature on page 53 based on data by EPICA community members 2004 and Siegenthaler et al 2005.

ISBN: 978 1 78908 076 6

Clipart from Corel®
Illustrations by: Sandy Gardner Artist, email sandy@sandygardner.co.uk
Printed by Elanders Ltd, Newcastle upon Tyne.

Based on the classic CGP style created by Richard Parsons.

Text, design, layout and original illustrations © Coordination Group Publications Ltd. (CGP) 2022
All rights reserved.

Photocopying this book is not permitted, even if you have a CLA licence.
Extra copies are available from CGP with next day delivery • 0800 1712 712 • www.cgpbooks.co.uk

Contents

✓ Use the tick boxes to check off the topics you've completed.

Topic 1 — Key Concepts in Chemistry
Atomic Structure and the Periodic Table............................1 ☐
Types of Bonding..3 ☐
Calculations Involving Masses...7 ☐

Topic 2 — States of Matter and Mixtures
States of Matter..11 ☐
Separating Mixtures..12 ☐
Water Treatment..15 ☐

Topic 3 — Chemical Changes
Acids...16 ☐
Electrolysis..18 ☐

Topic 4 — Extracting Metals and Equilibria
Metals and Sustainability..20 ☐
Reversible Reactions and Equilibria...............................26 ☐

Topic 5 — Separate Chemistry 1
Transition Metals, Alloys and Corrosion.......................28 ☐
Titrations...29 ☐
Atom Economy and Percentage Yield.............................31 ☐
Chemical Reactions in Industry.......................................33 ☐
Calculations with Gases...35 ☐
Chemical Cells and Fuel Cells...36 ☐

Topic 6 — Groups in the Periodic Table
Groups in the Periodic Table..42 ☐

Topic 7 — Rates of Reaction and Energy Changes
Rates of Reaction..45 ☐
Energy Changes...49 ☐

Topic 8 — Fuels and Earth Science
Fuels...51 ☐
Earth and Atmospheric Science.......................................53 ☐

Topic 9 — Separate Chemistry 2
Tests for Ions...56 ☐
Reactions of Organic Compounds...................................58 ☐
Polymers..60 ☐
Nanoparticles...61 ☐
Properties of Materials..64 ☐

Mixed Questions for Paper 2
Mixed Questions for Paper 2..68 ☐

Answers..74
Periodic Table..88

Mixed Questions for Paper 1
Mixed Questions for Paper 1..37 ☐

Exam Tips

Exam Basics

1) For Edexcel GCSE Chemistry, you'll sit <u>two exam papers</u> at the <u>end</u> of your course. Each exam will last <u>1 hour 45 minutes</u> and each paper will be worth <u>100 marks</u>.

2) <u>Paper 1</u> tests you on <u>Topics 1, 2, 3, 4 and 5</u>. <u>Paper 2</u> tests you on <u>Topics 1, 6, 7, 8 and 9</u>.

Be Prepared to be Tested on Your Maths and Practical Skills

1) Around <u>20% of the total marks</u> for Edexcel GCSE Chemistry come from questions that test your <u>maths skills</u>. The maths questions won't always be straightforward. For example, for some of the harder maths questions you might need to interpret some <u>tricky data</u> or do a <u>multi-step</u> calculation. If you're aiming for a top grade you need to make sure you're comfortable with all the maths skills you've used in your course.

2) Around <u>15% of the total marks</u> will be from questions testing <u>practical skills</u>. For example, you might be asked to comment on the <u>design</u> of an experiment (the <u>apparatus</u> and <u>methods</u>), make <u>predictions</u>, and <u>analyse</u> or <u>interpret results</u>. You can be tested on some of the <u>required practical activities</u> you'll have done as part of your course, but you'll also be expected to <u>apply</u> your practical knowledge to <u>unfamiliar experiments</u>.

Here are a Few Handy Hints

1) **Always, always, always make sure you <u>read the question properly</u>.**
This is a simple tip but it's really important. When you've got so much knowledge swimming round in your head it can be tempting to jump right in and start scribbling your answer down. But take time to make <u>absolutely sure</u> you're answering the question you've been asked.

2) **Take your <u>time</u> with <u>unfamiliar contexts</u>.**
Examiners like to test you really understand what you've learnt by asking you to apply your knowledge in <u>different ways</u>. Some of these contexts can be quite tricky but don't let them trip you up — read all the information you're given <u>really carefully</u> and, if you don't understand it, <u>read it again</u>. You can make notes alongside the question or underline certain bits if it helps you to focus on the <u>important</u> information.

3) **Look at the <u>number of marks</u> a question is worth.**
The number of marks gives you a pretty good clue as to <u>how much</u> to write. So if a question is worth four marks, make sure you write four decent points. And there's no point writing an essay for a question that's only worth one mark — it's just a waste of your time.

4) **Write your answers as <u>clearly</u> and <u>accurately</u> as you can.**
For <u>extended open response questions</u> (marked in this book with an asterisk, *) you'll be marked on the quality of your scientific reasoning. This means that as well as including <u>detailed</u> and <u>relevant</u> scientific information, you'll need to give your answer a <u>clear</u> and <u>logical structure</u> and show clearly how the ideas in it are <u>linked</u>.

5) **Show <u>each step</u> in your <u>calculations</u>.**
You might be a bit of a whizz at maths and be confident that your final answer to a question will be right, but everyone makes mistakes — especially when under the pressure of an exam. Always write things out in <u>steps</u> then, even if your final answer's wrong, you'll probably pick up <u>some marks</u> for your method.

6) **Pay attention to the <u>time</u>.**
After all those hours of revision it would be a shame to miss out on marks because you didn't have <u>time</u> to even attempt some of the questions. If you find that you're really struggling with a question, just <u>leave it</u> and <u>move on</u> to the next one. You can always <u>go back to it</u> at the end if you've got enough time.

These handy hints will help you pick up as many marks as you can in the exams — but they're no use if you haven't learnt the stuff in the first place. So make sure you revise well and do as many practice questions as you can.

Topic 1 — Key Concepts in Chemistry

Atomic Structure and the Periodic Table

1 This question is about a metallic element, **X**.

a) **Figure 1** shows the mass and relative abundance of different isotopes of element **X**.

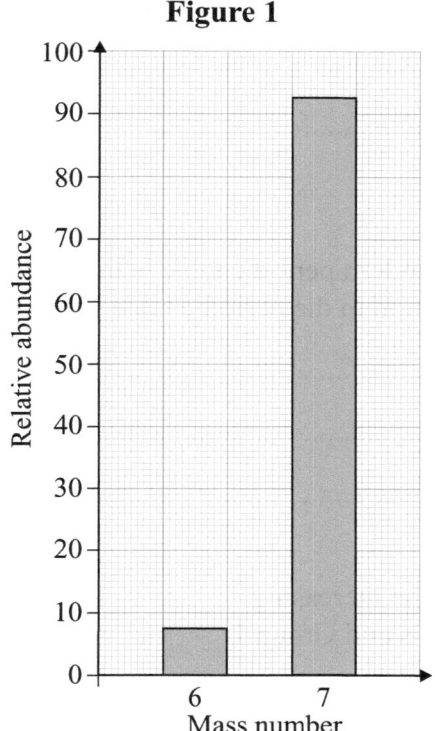

Calculate the relative atomic mass of **X**. Give your answer to **one** decimal place.
Give the name of the element.

Relative atomic mass = ... Name = ...
[4]

b) Give the electronic configuration of one particle of **X** present in XCl.

Electronic configuration = ...
[1]
[Total 5 marks]

2 Scientists once thought that atoms consisted of negatively charged particles within a positively charged 'pudding'.

Describe **two** ways in which our understanding of atomic structure has changed since this model.

....

....

....
[Total 2 marks]

3 This question is about the periodic table.

a) In 1869, Dmitri Mendeleev proposed a periodic table of the elements. His idea took several years to be accepted. The discovery of some new elements helped this to happen. Explain how the development of Mendeleev's table and its eventual acceptance show the scientific process at work.

....

....

....

....
[4]

b) The order of elements in the modern periodic table is linked to atomic structure.
Explain how aluminium's position in the periodic table is linked to the structure of its atoms.

....

....

....
[3]

c) The arrows in **Figure 2** show the increasing trend in reactivity of non-metals and Group 1 and Group 2 metals.

Figure 2

When metals and non-metals react, heat energy is given out.
The amount of heat energy given out increases with the reactivity of the reactants.
State which of the compounds below you would expect to give out the most heat energy when produced. Explain your reasoning.

    Caesium chloride   Caesium iodide   Sodium chloride   Sodium iodide

....

....

....

....
[3]
[Total 10 marks]

Exam Tip
A good knowledge of the atomic model and the periodic table will help you understand many other aspects of chemistry. You won't be expected to remember the dates of discoveries or who discovered them, but you need to understand the general ideas and how they demonstrate the scientific process.

Score: 17

Topic 1 — Key Concepts in Chemistry

Types of Bonding

1 This question is about ionic compounds.

a) Magnesium chloride is formed from magnesium and chlorine.
In terms of electron transfer, describe what happens when magnesium atoms react with chlorine atoms to form magnesium chloride.

....

....

....

....
[3]

b) In general, the larger the charges on the ions in an ionic compound, the stronger the ionic bonding. Use this information to compare the melting point of magnesium oxide with the melting point of sodium chloride. Explain your answer.

....

....

....

....
[3]

Figure 1 shows a representation of the structure of caesium chloride.

Figure 1

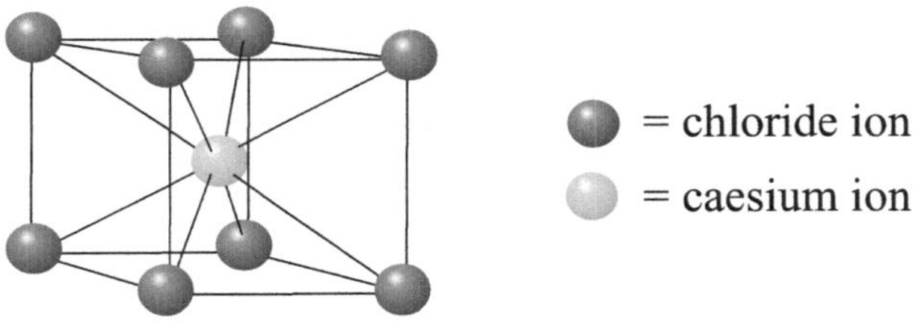

● = chloride ion
○ = caesium ion

c) State **one** advantage and **one** disadvantage of using the type of diagram in **Figure 1** to represent the structure of caesium chloride.

Advantage: ....

Disadvantage: ....
[2]

d) Write a balanced symbol equation for the formation of caesium chloride from its elements.

....
[2]

[Total 10 marks]

Topic 1 — Key Concepts in Chemistry

2   A student is investigating the electrical conductivity of calcium chloride in various states. **Figure 2** shows the circuit that she uses.

Figure 2

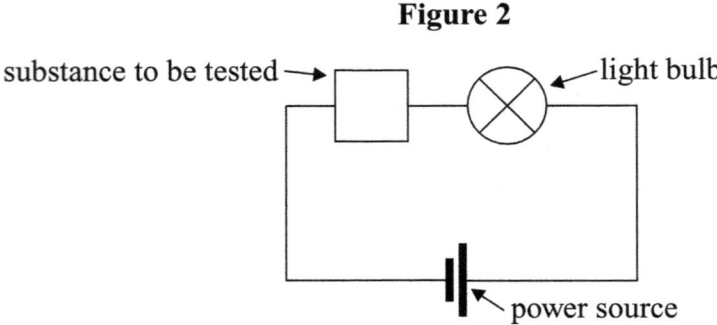

The student tests calcium chloride as both a solid and as an aqueous solution. Predict the results of each experiment. Explain your answers.

Solid: ....

....

Aqueous: ....

....

[Total 4 marks]

3* Metals and graphite have similarities and differences in their structure and their properties. Compare and contrast the structure and properties of metals and graphite. In your answer you should explain how the properties of both relate to their structure and bonding.

....

....

....

....

....

....

....

....

....

....

....

....

[Total 6 marks]

Topic 1 — Key Concepts in Chemistry

4 Fluorine will react with a Group 1 element to form a fluoride compound. Describe and explain how fluorine's bonding changes during this reaction.

....
....
....
....
....
....
....

[Total 4 marks]

5 **Figure 3** shows the structure of silicon dioxide.

Figure 3

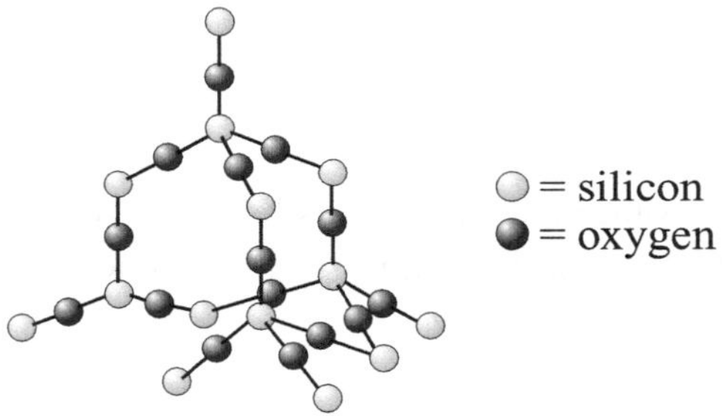

○ = silicon
● = oxygen

Silicon dioxide

a)* Use **Figure 3** and your own knowledge of the bonding in diamond to describe the similarities and differences between the structures of diamond and silicon dioxide.

....
....
....
....
....
....
....
....

[6]

Topic 1 — Key Concepts in Chemistry

b) Diamond is an extremely hard substance. State whether you would expect silicon dioxide to be a hard substance like diamond. Explain your answer.

....

....

....
[2]

c) Graphene is a form of the element carbon.
Draw a diagram to show the structure of graphene.
Label the value of the angle made by adjacent carbon-carbon bonds.

[2]
[Total 10 marks]

6   Covalent compounds contain strong bonds between their atoms. Explain why some covalent compounds have very low melting points while some have very high melting points.

....

....

....

....

....

....

....

....
[Total 4 marks]

Exam Tip

If you're stuck answering a question about the bonds or structure of an element or compound, try drawing a quick sketch of the atoms, ions or molecules involved. You could also consider the electronic configuration of the elements and think about how this determines the bonds that form.

Score: 38

Topic 1 — Key Concepts in Chemistry

Calculations Involving Masses

1 "Fizzy sherbet" contains citric acid ($C_6H_8O_7$) and sodium hydrogencarbonate ($NaHCO_3$). When water is added to fizzy sherbet, the citric acid and the sodium hydrogencarbonate react to form carbon dioxide, water and sodium citrate ($C_6H_5O_7Na_3$).

The equation for this reaction is:

$$C_6H_8O_{7(s)} + 3NaHCO_{3(s)} \rightarrow 3CO_{2(g)} + 3H_2O_{(l)} + C_6H_5O_7Na_{3(aq)}$$

A student tested two brands of fizzy sherbet by mixing 10 g of each type with water in an open flask. She measured the mass of each flask and its contents at the start and end of the reaction.

a) Explain why a decrease in mass was expected.

....

....
[1]

b) The student tested the pH of the colourless solution in each flask at the end of the experiment. She concluded that unreacted citric acid was present in one of the flasks.
State which of the reactants limited the amount of product formed in this case.
Explain your answer.

....

....

....

....
[2]

c) The student decided to make her own fizzy sherbet using 20.0 g of citric acid. Calculate the minimum mass of sodium hydrogencarbonate needed to ensure all of the citric acid is used up in the reaction. Give your answer to three significant figures.
Relative formula masses (M_r): $NaHCO_3$ = 84; $C_6H_8O_7$ = 192

Mass = ... g
[3]

Topic 1 — Key Concepts in Chemistry

d) Another student repeated the reaction between citric acid and sodium hydrogencarbonate, but used different quantities of reactants. At the end of the reaction the water was evaporated and a 61.15 g sample of sodium citrate was collected. Use the reaction equation to calculate the mass of citric acid that reacted. Give your answer to three significant figures.
Relative formula mass (M_r) of $C_6H_8O_7$ = 192
Relative atomic masses (A_r): H = 1; C = 12; O = 16; Na = 23

Mass = ... g
[4]
[Total 10 marks]

2 A student is investigating the effects of two different catalysts on a reaction.
One of the catalysts is manganese dioxide (MnO_2, M_r = 87.0).
The other is a catalyst with the formula XO_a (M_r = 79.5), where X is a metal.
Both catalysts are powders.

a) The student uses 1.74 g of MnO_2 in his experiment. In order to make it a fair test, the same number of moles of XO_a is also used. Calculate the mass of XO_a required.

Mass = ... g
[2]

b) The catalyst XO_a can be made by reacting metal X with oxygen gas.
3.55 g of oxygen gas reacted with metal X to form 17.65 g of XO_a. There were no other products.
Use this information to balance the symbol equation below, and then work out the value of a.
You must show your working.
Relative formula mass (M_r) of O_2 = 32

Balanced symbol equation: .... X + ... O_2 → .... XO_a

a = ...
[4]
[Total 6 marks]

Topic 1 — Key Concepts in Chemistry

3 Sodium hydrogencarbonate, NaHCO$_3$, is an important ingredient in baking powder. It gives off carbon dioxide when added to acidic liquids, such as vinegar. A student adds different volumes of vinegar to six beakers, each containing the same mass of NaHCO$_3$, and measures the mass loss of the reaction mixture, due to the production of CO$_2$. **Figure 1** shows the results.

Figure 1

Volume of vinegar (cm^3)	Mass loss (g)
10	1.0
20	1.3
30	1.6
40	1.8
50	2.0
60	2.0

a) Explain why the mass eventually stops decreasing, despite more vinegar being added.

....

....
[1]

b) Suggest **one** way in which the student could adapt their method to give a more accurate indication of the minimum volume of vinegar required to reduce the mass by 2.0 g.

....

....
[1]

c) Baking powder is a mixture of sodium hydrogencarbonate, NaHCO$_3$, and tartaric acid, C$_4$H$_6$O$_6$. The equation for the reaction between sodium hydrogencarbonate and tartaric acid is:

$$2NaHCO_3 + C_4H_6O_6 \rightarrow 2CO_2 + 2H_2O + C_4H_4O_6Na_2$$

The reaction is carried out using 12.9 g of sodium hydrogencarbonate and 14.1 g of tartaric acid. Sodium hydrogencarbonate is the limiting reactant.

Calculate the mass of tartaric acid that will be left over once the reaction is complete.
Give your answer to two significant figures.
Relative formula masses (M_r): NaHCO$_3$ = 84; C$_4$H$_6$O$_6$ = 150

Mass = ... g
[4]

[Total 6 marks]

Topic 1 — Key Concepts in Chemistry

4 Sucrose has the chemical formula $C_{12}H_{22}O_{11}$. Sucrose can react as follows:

Equation 1: $C_{12}H_{22}O_{11} + 12O_2 \rightarrow 12CO_2 + 11H_2O$ (complete combustion)

Equation 2: $C_{12}H_{22}O_{11} + nO_2 \rightarrow xCO + yCO_2 + 11H_2O$ (incomplete combustion)

Equation 3: $C_{12}H_{22}O_{11} \rightarrow 12C + 11H_2O$ (decomposition)

Relative formula masses (M_r): $C_{12}H_{22}O_{11} = 342$; $CO_2 = 44$; $CO = 28$; $H_2O = 18$;
Relative atomic mass (A_r) of C = 12

a) Use **Equation 1** to calculate the number of moles of carbon dioxide that will be produced from the complete combustion of 6.84 g of sucrose. Tick **one** box.

☐ A 10.56 moles of carbon dioxide
☐ B 44 moles of carbon dioxide
☐ C 0.24 moles of carbon dioxide
☐ D 6.86 moles of carbon dioxide

[1]

b) A student burns 5.13 g of sucrose in a sealed container to ensure incomplete combustion. 3.36 g of CO and 2.64 g of CO_2 are produced. Use this information to write **Equation 2** as a balanced equation.

Balanced symbol equation: $C_{12}H_{22}O_{11}$ + ... O_2 → .... CO + ... CO_2 + 11H_2O

[5]

c) Another student strongly heats a sample of sucrose until a black residue of carbon remains. Use **Equation 3** to calculate the mass of carbon that could be produced from 12.0 g of sucrose. Give your answer to an appropriate number of significant figures.

Mass = ... g

[3]

[Total 9 marks]

Exam Tip
The hardest part of mass calculations is rearranging the formulas. Once that's done, just use your calculator to do the maths. Always remember to give your answer to the correct number of significant figures — forgetting to do this can be a really easy way to lose out on marks.

Score: ⬜ / 31

Topic 1 — Key Concepts in Chemistry

Topic 2 — States of Matter and Mixtures

States of Matter

1 Particle theory can be used to explain changes of state.

[margin note: bonds between particles weakened → overcome forces/bonds]

a) Use particle theory to explain what happens to the particles in a solid when it melts.

When a solid melts, initially the particles vibrate around a point *and* have bonds between them but as it is heated the particles gain kinetic energy *& vibrate more* and the bonds start to break *weakened* due to the forces of attraction being overcome *at melting point* → particles then can move around one another once it is a liquid. [4] ③

b) Suggest **one** benefit and **one** drawback of using the particle model to explain changes of state.

Benefit: compare arrangement of particles in each state of matter

Drawback: particles shown as solid inelastic spheres

[2]

[Total 6 marks]

2* Above 80 °C, sodium hydrogencarbonate (NaHCO$_3$) breaks down into a number of products, including carbon dioxide gas. CO_2
At −78.5 °C, dry ice (solid carbon dioxide) sublimes to become carbon dioxide gas.

Explain which of these processes is most easily reversible and why.

Sublimation is a physical change and so can be *more easily* reversed whereas decomposition of sodium hydrogencarbonate is a chemical change, so is more difficult to reverse. To reverse the sublimation of dry ice, you have to do deposition.

[margin: deposition = gas→solid]

In a physical process: the bonds are broken *between molecules* as they have enough energy to be overcome & all the particles are unchanged chemically, so by reducing the *temp.* energy, the bonds can re-form. *substances remain the same*

In a chemical process: the substances (reactants) are changed ③ chemically to produce different products. ✓ ∴ are harder to change back → bonds between atoms break, new bonds → requires several steps, form between atoms of reactants to produce different substance/products

[Total 6 marks]

> **Exam Tip**
> In this last question, you're asked to provide an explanation, not just a description of what's going on. This means your answer will have to include a conclusion that is supported by what you write.

Score: 12

Separating Mixtures

1 A scientist is separating some mixtures of substances.

a) The first mixture is of copper sulfate, silicon dioxide and water.
Copper sulfate is soluble in water.
Silicon dioxide is a giant covalent substance which is insoluble in water.

Name **two** techniques that could be used as part of a two-step process to purify each of the copper sulfate and silicon dioxide from the mixture with water. Explain why each technique is suitable.

Technique 1: ....

Explanation: ....

....

Technique 2: ....

Explanation: ....

....

[4]

b) A second mixture consists of three liquids with boiling points of 50 °C, 65 °C and 80 °C. Explain why fractional distillation is needed and how it can be used to separate these substances.

....

....

....

....

....

....

[4]

c) The third mixture contains a complex set of liquids that will react together if heated. Name a suitable separation technique. Explain your reasoning.

Technique: ....

Explanation: ....

....

....

[2]

[Total 10 marks]

2 A medicine comes in a 5.0 g sachet. It contains 120 mg of paracetamol per 5.0 g, along with various other ingredients.

a) Calculate the percentage of paracetamol in each sachet.

.... %
[2]

b) The medicine contains several compounds called parabens. A sample of the medicine, along with pure samples of four parabens, was analysed by paper chromatography.

Explain how paper chromatography separates out the substances in the medicine.
Do not include details of how you would carry out the practical in your answer.

....
....
....
....
....
[3]

The resulting chromatogram is shown in **Figure 1**.

Figure 1

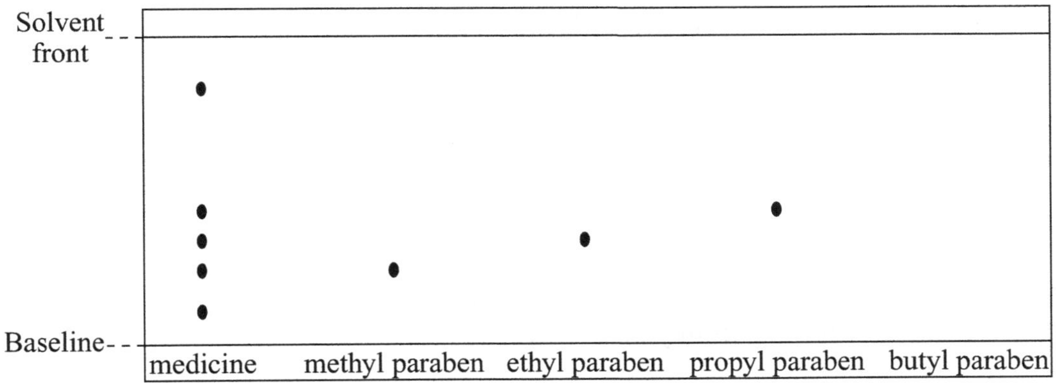

c) Calculate the R_f value for propyl paraben.
Give your answer to an appropriate number of significant figures.

R_f = ...
[3]

Topic 2 — States of Matter and Mixtures

d) The R_f value for butyl paraben, which is not found in the medicine, is 0.52.
Calculate the distance moved by butyl paraben on the chromatogram.
Mark its position on **Figure 1**.

Distance = ... cm
[3]

e) A sample of ethanol is thought to be contaminated with ethyl paraben.
When separated from the ethanol, the contaminating substance was found to have a melting point of 115-120 °C.

What does this information suggest about the purity of the contaminant? Explain your answer.

....

....
[2]
[Total 13 marks]

3 A compound, **Z**, is believed to be contaminated with an unknown impurity.

a) Explain the difference between the everyday and scientific definitions of 'pure'.

....

....
[1]

b) The impurity is believed to be one of substances **A**, **B** or **C**.
Describe how a paper chromatography experiment can be used to help identify which, if any, of the impurities is present in compound **Z**.

....

....

....
[2]

c) Describe how you could use further paper chromatography experiments to confirm any conclusions from your first result.

....

....
[2]
[Total 5 marks]

Exam Tip

Think about the physical properties of the substances within a mixture to decide how they might be separated out. If a mixture described in an exam question contains several substances, then there's a good chance you'll need to use more than one technique to separate them all.

Score: ☐ / 28

Topic 2 — States of Matter and Mixtures

Water Treatment

1. A mining company uses large volumes of water to process metal ores. Afterwards, the water must be cleaned before it can be returned to the environment.

   a) Give the names of **two** methods the company could use to clean the water.

   ....
   [2]

   b) Scientists at the mine were found to be using tap water during the chemical analysis of ore specimens. Explain how this might have affected their results and name an alternative to tap water that the scientists could use instead.

   ....

   ....

   ....
   [3]

   c)* The mining company uses ground water to process ore. It wants to reduce its use of ground water, and puts forward the following options for obtaining the water required:
   - Use of waste water from other processes in the mine.
   - Distillation of seawater.

   Evaluate the two options and suggest which option the company should adopt. You should justify any conclusion you make.

   ....

   ....

   ....

   ....

   ....

   ....

   ....

   ....

   ....

   ....
   [6]
   [Total 11 marks]

> **Exam Tip**
> The word evaluate in this last question means review the information you've been given and form a conclusion based upon the advantages and disadvantages of the options. As well as using your knowledge of chemistry, keep in mind the practicality of the options (e.g. how much it would cost?).
>
> Score: 11

Topic 2 — States of Matter and Mixtures

Topic 3 — Chemical Changes

Acids

1 The pH values of three acidic solutions are shown in **Figure 1**.

Figure 1

Acid	Sulfuric acid	Oxalic acid	Boric acid
pH	1	3	6

a) Identify the acid which has the lowest concentration of H⁺ ions in solution.

....
[1]

b) What does the difference in the pH values for the sulfuric acid and the oxalic acid tell you about the difference in their H⁺ ion concentrations?

....

....
[1]

c) A solution of oxalic acid was heated. Its volume decreased.
Assuming that only water was evaporated, explain the effect on the pH of the solution.

....

....
[2]

[Total 4 marks]

2 A scientist has a 25 cm³ solution of 1 mol dm⁻³ carbonic acid, a weak acid.
He also has a 25 cm³ solution of 1 mol dm⁻³ perchloric acid, a strong acid.

a) Which of the following statements is true? Tick **one** box.

☐ **A** The pH of the carbonic acid solution is higher than the pH of the perchloric acid solution.

☐ **B** The carbonic acid solution contains a higher proportion of water molecules than the perchloric acid solution.

☐ **C** The perchloric acid solution is more concentrated than the carbonic acid solution.

☐ **D** The carbonic acid solution contains fewer acid molecules than the perchloric acid solution.

[1]

b) Describe how the concentration of hydrogen ions in the solution of carbonic acid compares to the concentration of acid molecules. Explain your answer.

....

....

....
[2]

[Total 3 marks]

3 This question is about the reactions of acids.

a) Dilute hydrochloric acid is added to a flask containing an unknown solid substance. A reaction occurs. The only products of the reaction are sodium chloride and hydrogen gas.

  i) Suggest the identity of the unknown solid substance.

  ....
  [1]

  ii) Describe how you could confirm the identity of the gas.

  ....
  ....
  [2]

b) A student has two flasks containing the same volume of 0.5 mol dm^{-3} nitric acid, HNO$_3$. She adds some magnesium hydroxide to the first flask and the same mass of magnesium carbonate to the second flask.

  i) Write a balanced equation for the reaction between magnesium hydroxide and nitric acid.

  ....
  [2]

  ii) State and explain **one** difference that the student will observe between the two reactions.

  ....
  ....
  [2]

  iii) Give **one** other reagent that the student could have added to the first flask instead of magnesium hydroxide that would produce the same two products.

  ....
  [1]

c) Another student has a solid metal compound, **MX**. He adds a sample of **MX** to a beaker of deionised water and stirs. No solid residue can be seen in the beaker.

  The student then measures the pH of a solution of sulfuric acid. He adds a sample of solid **MX** to the sulfuric acid. The pH of the solution increases. No bubbles are produced. State and explain what this tells you about the nature of the metal compound, **MX**.

  ....
  ....
  ....
  ....
  [4]

  [Total 12 marks]

Topic 3 — Chemical Changes

Electrolysis

1 Which row of the table correctly shows the products of the electrolysis of molten magnesium chloride? Tick **one** box.

	Product at anode	Product at cathode
A	Oxygen	Magnesium
B	Chlorine	Magnesium
C	Chlorine	Hydrogen
D	Magnesium	Chlorine

[Total 1 mark]

2 This question is about the electrolysis of aqueous copper sulfate, $CuSO_4$, using inert electrodes.

a) Draw a labelled diagram showing the set-up of the apparatus needed for the electrolysis of aqueous copper sulfate using inert electrodes. Label the anode and the cathode.

[2]

b) State what products are formed at each electrode. Explain why these products are formed.

....
....
....
....
....
[4]

c) Write half equations for the reactions occurring at the anode and the cathode.

Anode: ....

Cathode: ....
[2]

d) Identify the species that is reduced in this electrolysis. Explain your answer.

Species: ....

Explanation: ....
[2]

[Total 10 marks]

Topic 3 — Chemical Changes

3 A cell is constructed using an electrolyte and graphite electrodes.
Gaseous products are formed at both the anode and the cathode.

a) Which of the following electrolytes could **not** have been used in the cell? Tick **one** box.

☐ **A** Molten zinc chloride
☐ **B** Dilute sulfuric acid
☐ **C** Aqueous potassium sulfate
☐ **D** Aqueous sodium chloride

[1]

b) At one of the electrodes, an aqueous ion loses electrons to become a gaseous element.
State which electrode this reaction occurred at. Explain your answer in terms of redox.

....

....
[2]
[Total 3 marks]

4* Sodium can be extracted from sodium hydroxide using electrolysis.

Using your knowledge of electrolysis, suggest how this method could be used to extract sodium from solid sodium hydroxide. Your answer should include any other products formed and the half equations for the reactions at both electrodes.

....
....
....
....
....
....
....
....
....
....
....

[Total 6 marks]

Exam Tip
Half equations crop up quite a bit in electrolysis, so you need to be confident at writing them. Remember, just like in a full equation, you need the same atoms and equal charges on both sides — but you should only have electrons on one side, showing a reactant being oxidised or reduced.

Score: ▢ / 20

Topic 3 — Chemical Changes

Topic 4 — Extracting Metals and Equilibria

Metals and Sustainability

1 Titanium and its alloys are useful materials due to their strength, low density and resistance to corrosion. However, their use is limited by the high cost of titanium extraction.

a) Use the reactivity series in **Figure 1** to suggest **one** reason why titanium is a suitable material for pipes that transport sea water.

....

....
[1]

Figure 1

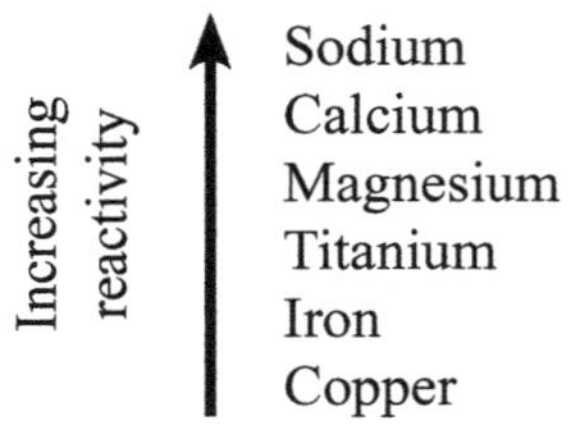

Increasing reactivity ↑
Sodium
Calcium
Magnesium
Titanium
Iron
Copper

b) The most common ores of titanium are rutile, TiO_2, and ilmenite, $FeTiO_3$. Suggest **one** reason why it might be preferable to extract titanium from rutile, even though rutile is less abundant and more expensive than ilmenite.

....
[1]

Figure 2 shows the process of extracting titanium from rutile.

Figure 2

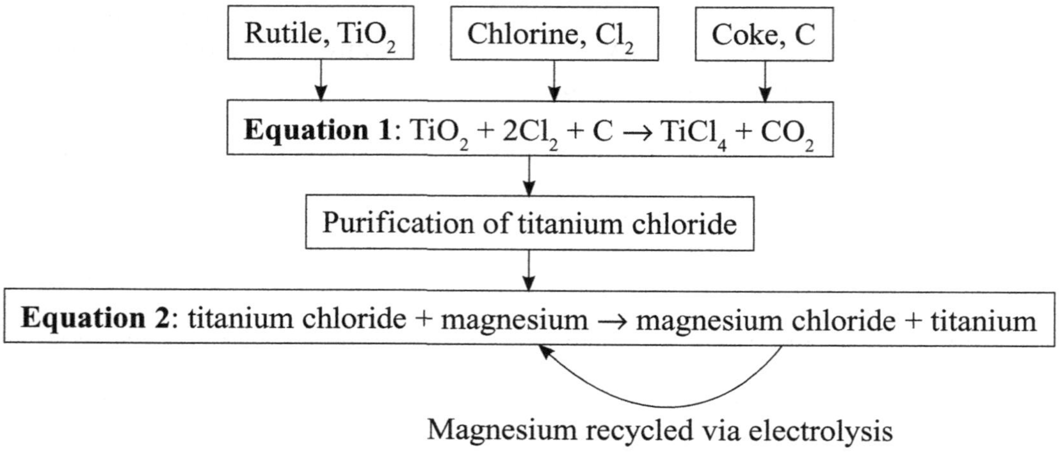

Rutile, TiO_2 | Chlorine, Cl_2 | Coke, C
↓
Equation 1: $TiO_2 + 2Cl_2 + C \rightarrow TiCl_4 + CO_2$
↓
Purification of titanium chloride
↓
Equation 2: titanium chloride + magnesium → magnesium chloride + titanium

Magnesium recycled via electrolysis

c) Use **Figure 2** to suggest **two** reasons why the extraction of titanium is expensive.

1. ....

2. ....
[2]

d) i) Write a balanced symbol equation for **Equation 2**.

....
[2]

ii) Identify the species that are oxidised and reduced in the reaction in **Equation 2**.

Oxidised: ....

Reduced: ....
[2]

[Total 8 marks]

2 This question is about the reactivity of metals.

Zinc reacts with cold, dilute hydrochloric acid. The equation for the reaction is:

$$Zn + 2HCl \rightarrow ZnCl_2 + H_2$$

a) i) Predict what would occur if copper was used instead of zinc. Explain your answer.

....

....
[2]

ii) Write a balanced ionic equation for the reaction between zinc and hydrochloric acid.

....
[1]

iii) Identify the species that gains electrons in the reaction between zinc and hydrochloric acid.

....
[1]

b) When magnesium is added to blue copper sulfate solution ($CuSO_4$), a reaction occurs in which the colour of the solution fades and an orange-brown solid is formed on the magnesium. Write a balanced symbol equation for this reaction. Include state symbols.
Use your equation to explain the observations made.

Equation: ....

Explanation: ....

....

....
[4]

c) Displacement reactions give out heat energy.
Use **Figure 1** to suggest an explanation why the amount of heat energy given out by the reaction between calcium and magnesium nitrate is only very small.

....

....
[1]

d) **Figure 3** shows the results of adding three different metals to water and to dilute hydrochloric acid.

Figure 3

Metal	X	Y	Z
Reaction with water	Slight fizzing	No reaction	Fizzing
Reaction with dilute acid	Fizzing	No reaction	Vigorous fizzing

Which of the following is true? Tick **one** box.

☐ **A** Metal X could displace metal Y from a solution of metal Y's salt.

☐ **B** The order of reactivity is Y < Z < X.

☐ **C** Metal Z is near the bottom of the reactivity series

☐ **D** Metal X will not react with steam.
[1]

[Total 10 marks]

Topic 4 — Extracting Metals and Equilibria

3 A plumbing supplies company makes copper pipes. They consider two different methods for sourcing the copper: reduction of copper ores and bioleaching.

Figure 4 shows some data about the two sources of copper.

Figure 4

Source	Reduction of copper ores	Bioleaching
Materials	Requires high-grade copper ores, large volumes of water and a reducing agent, e.g. carbon.	Low-grade copper ores can be used. Naturally-forming, recyclable bacteria and an acidic environment are also used.
Method	Many-step process that involves the crushing, grinding and high-temperature heating of ores.	Bacteria separate the copper from its ore in a slow process that can be carried out at low temperatures.
Waste	Low-grade ores that are unsuitable for reduction are disposed of. Processes produce carbon dioxide, carbon monoxide and sulfur dioxide.	Acidic waste can be produced. All products end up in aqueous solution.

a)* Using the information in **Figure 4**, evaluate the environmental impact of using each source of copper.

....
....
....
....
....
....
....
....
....
....
....
....

[6]

b) Give **one** economic advantage of sourcing copper from the reduction of copper ores.

....

[1]

[Total 7 marks]

Exam Tip

The reactivity series is a great tool for understanding the reactivity of metals, so make sure you know how to use it. By looking at the relative positions of a metal, carbon and hydrogen you can work out if the metal can be reduced by carbon and whether or not the metal will react with dilute acids.

Topic 4 — Extracting Metals and Equilibria

Target AO3

4   Figure 5, Figure 6 and Figure 7 contain information about the reactivities of different metals. The oxidation potential data in Figure 5 can be used as a measure of how easily an element can be oxidised. For each half equation, the higher the oxidation potential, the more easily the element on the left-hand side will lose electrons.

Figure 5

Oxidation Reaction	Oxidation Potential
Ni → Ni^{2+} + 2e$^-$	0.25
Ca → Ca^{2+} + 2e$^-$	2.87
Pb → Pb^{2+} + 2e$^-$	0.13

Figure 6

Metal	Method of Extraction
Calcium	Electrolysis
Aluminium	Electrolysis
Iron	Reduction with carbon
Barium	Electrolysis

Figure 7

Reaction with Dilute Acid	Observation
Pb + 2HCl → PbCl$_2$ + H$_2$	Extremely slow reaction
Ca + 2HCl → CaCl$_2$ + H$_2$	Vigorous fizzing
2Al + 6HCl → 2AlCl$_3$ + 3H$_2$	Some fizzing
Ba + 2HCl → BaCl$_2$ + H$_2$	Very vigorous fizzing

a) Use the information given in the tables above to place nickel, aluminium, lead and barium into the reactivity series below.

Reactivity Series
....
Calcium
....
Iron
....
....

[3]

b) Using the information in Figure 6, suggest where carbon would be placed in the reactivity series above. Explain your answer.

....

....

....

[3]

[Total 6 marks]

Topic 4 — Extracting Metals and Equilibria

Target AO3

5 A company uses a process called the Dow process to extract magnesium from sea water.
Figure 8 contains some information about the Dow process.

Figure 8

Cost	High, as large amounts of electricity are required.
Purity of end product	Produces a very pure product.
Other products	Chlorine is also produced. It is used to make hydrochloric acid, which is a reactant in the Dow process.

a) Suggest the method of metal extraction that is used in the Dow process.

....
[1]

b) Identify **one** way that the company reduces the amount of waste created by the process.

....

....
[1]
[Total 2 marks]

6 A mining company is exploring more environmentally-friendly ways of extracting copper.
Figure 9 contains information on two sustainable methods of extracting copper.

Figure 9

Factor	Phytoextraction	Bioleaching
Cost	Currently more expensive than mining.	More cost-effective than mining.
Environmental impact	Reduces noise pollution and habitat loss. Involves burning plants, which produces greenhouse gases.	Reduces noise pollution and habitat loss. Produces toxic waste products.
Rate of extraction	Slow	Slow

Evaluate the two methods and suggest which option the company should use.
You should use **Figure 9** to justify any conclusion you make.

....

....

....

....

....

....
[Total 4 marks]

Topic 4 — Extracting Metals and Equilibria

Target AO3

7 A student is given life cycle assessments for a traditional plastic bottle made from crude oil, and a new biodegradable bottle made from bioplastic. Bioplastic is a type of plastic made from biological material. The life cycle assessments are shown in **Figure 10**.

Figure 10

	Bioplastic bottle	**Traditional plastic bottle**
Raw Materials	Waste cooking oil and bacteria	Crude oil
Manufacturing	Bacteria process waste cooking oil to produce polyester molecules which can then be used to make bioplastics.	Crude oil is refined. The resulting compounds are polymerised and processed in several energy-intensive steps.
Usage	Can be reused	Can be reused
Disposal	Can biodegrade but requires specific conditions that aren't always met	Cannot biodegrade

The student concluded that, "The assessments show that bioplastic bottles are significantly better for the environment than traditional plastic bottles made from crude oil."

a)* Evaluate how well the information in **Figure 10** supports the student's conclusion.

....
....
....
....
....
....
....
....
....

[6]

b) It is also possible to produce bioplastics from crops grown specifically for this purpose. Suggest how using crops, instead of waste cooking oil, to produce the bioplastic might negatively affect the LCA of the bottle.

....
....
....
....

[2]

[Total 8 marks]

Score: ☐

44

Topic 4 — Extracting Metals and Equilibria

Reversible Reactions and Equilibria

1 Gaseous iodine is a purple vapour. It reacts with hydrogen gas in a reversible reaction to produce a colourless gas, hydrogen iodide.

The equation for the reaction is: $I_{2(g)} + H_{2(g)} \rightleftharpoons 2HI_{(g)}$

a) Explain how equilibrium is reached when gaseous iodine reacts with hydrogen gas in a closed system.

....

....

....

....

....

[3]

b) Explain what would happen to the position of the equilibrium if the concentration of gaseous iodine was increased.

....

....

[2]

Figure 1 shows how the masses of iodine and hydrogen iodide change with time.

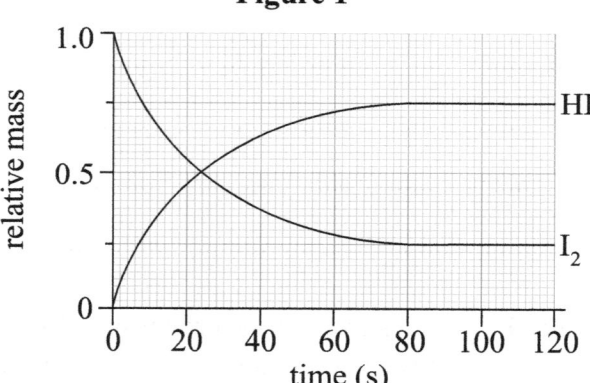

Figure 1

c) Determine the time at which equilibrium is reached.   Time = ... s

[1]

d) What would you observe if hydrogen gas was removed from the system and all other conditions remained the same? Tick **one** box.

☐ **A** More purple vapour

☐ **B** An increase in the total volume of gas

☐ **C** No visible change

☐ **D** Less purple vapour

[1]

Topic 4 — Extracting Metals and Equilibria

e) A test tube containing iodine, hydrogen gas and hydrogen iodide was sealed and placed in an ice bath. After a few seconds, the reaction mixture was found to contain more purple vapour. Explain what this suggests about the backwards reaction.

....

....

....

....

[3]

[Total 10 marks]

2   The Contact process is used for the manufacture of sulfuric acid.

The second stage in the process is a reversible reaction. The equation for this reaction is:

$$2SO_{2(g)} + O_{2(g)} \rightleftharpoons 2SO_{3(g)}$$

Figure 2 shows how the percentage yield of sulfur trioxide (SO$_3$) changes with temperature.

Figure 2

Percentage yield of sulfur trioxide, SO$_3$ (%) vs Temperature (°C)

Use the information in the question and your own knowledge to explain the conditions of temperature and pressure that would give the maximum percentage yield of SO$_3$.

....

....

....

....

....

....

....

[Total 4 marks]

Exam Tip
If you're asked about a reversible reaction, pay close attention to the reaction equation.
It can help you to figure out the effects of changing conditions like concentration and pressure.
Remember, dynamic equilibrium is only reached when the reaction is carried out in a <u>closed</u> system.

Score:

14

Topic 4 — Extracting Metals and Equilibria

Topic 5 — Separate Chemistry 1

Transition Metals, Alloys and Corrosion

1   This question is about the properties of materials.

Part of the reactivity series of metals is shown in **Figure 1**.

Figure 1

Potassium
Sodium
Calcium
Magnesium   Decreasing reactivity
Zinc
Iron
Copper

a) Use **Figure 1** to suggest which of these metals would be the most suitable material for water storage tanks. Explain your answer.

....
....
[2]

b)* The hull of a ship is made of steel and has magnesium blocks attached to it. Use your knowledge and **Figure 1** to compare and contrast the use of magnesium blocks with other methods of preventing corrosion. Include in your answer why magnesium is a good choice for the blocks.

....
....
....
....
....
....
....
....
....
....
[6]

c) Aluminium corrodes when exposed to air containing oxygen and water. Aluminium oxide forms and acts as a protective layer, sticking to the aluminium below it. Compare the corrosion of iron and aluminium in air.

....
....
....
[3]

[Total 11 marks]

Exam Tip

You could be given a question about a transition metal you've never heard of before. Don't worry — unless it says otherwise in the question, the metal will have the same standard properties as the transition metals you do know. You'll be expected to be able to recall these properties in the exam.

Score:

11

Topic 5 — Separate Chemistry 1

Titrations

1 A student carried out a titration using sulfuric acid to determine the concentration of a solution of sodium hydroxide.

The equation for the reaction is:

$$2NaOH_{(aq)} + H_2SO_{4(aq)} \rightarrow Na_2SO_{4(aq)} + 2H_2O_{(l)}$$

This is the method used:

1. Measure out 25 cm³ of sulfuric acid and pour it into a conical flask.
2. Add a few drops of indicator to the conical flask.
3. Fill a burette with sodium hydroxide solution.
4. Record the initial volume of sodium hydroxide solution in the burette.
5. Add the sodium hydroxide solution from the burette to the sulfuric acid and record the volume at the point when the indicator changes colour.
6. Calculate the total volume added.
7. Repeat until results within 0.1 cm³ are obtained.

The student's results are shown in **Figure 1**.

Figure 1

Volume of NaOH solution (cm³)	Titration 1	Titration 2	Titration 3
Initial reading	0.00	24.50	0.20
Final reading	24.50	49.70	25.50
Volume added	24.50	25.20	25.30

a) What was the mean volume of sodium hydroxide solution added?
Ignore any anomalous results. Tick **one** box.

☐ **A** 25.0 cm³ ☐ **B** 25.00 cm³ ☐ **C** 25.25 cm³ ☐ **D** 25.30 cm³

[1]

b) In a second experiment, 23.40 cm³ of sodium hydroxide solution was required to neutralise 25.0 cm³ of 0.500 mol dm⁻³ sulfuric acid.
Calculate the concentration of the sodium hydroxide solution in mol dm⁻³.
Give your answer to three significant figures.

Concentration = ... mol dm⁻³

[3]

[Total 4 marks]

Topic 5 — Separate Chemistry 1

2 An unknown mass of sodium hydroxide was used to make 25 cm³ of sodium hydroxide solution. This solution was neutralised by 0.25 mol dm⁻³ hydrochloric acid in a titration.

a) The pH of the solution was measured throughout the titration. The results are shown in **Figure 2**. Determine the volume of hydrochloric acid required to neutralise the sodium hydroxide solution.

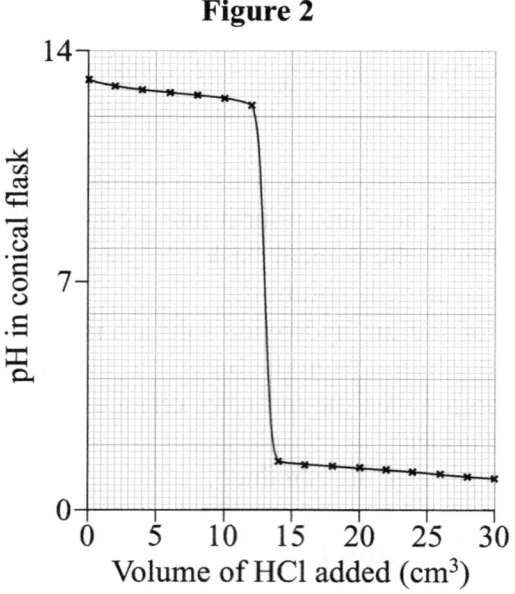

Volume = ... cm³
[1]

b) A different mass of sodium hydroxide was used to make another 25 cm³ solution. 35 cm³ of 0.25 mol dm⁻³ hydrochloric acid was required to neutralise this solution. Calculate the mass of sodium hydroxide in the 25 cm³ solution that was used in the titration. Relative formula mass (M_r) of NaOH = 40

Mass = ... g
[4]

[Total 5 marks]

Exam Tip
If you're given the concentration and volume of a solution, or the mass and M_r (or A_r) of a substance, you'll often need to calculate the number of moles. Finding the number of moles can be a good way to start if you're stuck, and it'll give you a chance of picking up a mark or two.

Score: 9

Topic 5 — Separate Chemistry 1

Atom Economy and Percentage Yield

1. A student makes hydrated copper sulfate crystals via the three-step process shown below:

   Step 1: Heat copper carbonate until it forms copper oxide.
   $$CuCO_{3(s)} \rightarrow CuO_{(s)} + CO_{2(g)}$$
   Step 2: Add an excess of copper oxide to sulfuric acid until all the acid has reacted.
   $$CuO_{(s)} + H_2SO_{4(aq)} \rightarrow CuSO_{4(aq)} + H_2O_{(l)}$$
   Step 3: Filter the solution and heat the filtrate until most of the water has evaporated. Leave the remaining water to evaporate until crystallisation occurs.

   Relative formula masses (M_r): CuO = 79.5; H_2SO_4 = 98; $CuSO_4$ = 159.5; H_2O = 18.

   a) 12.0 g of $CuCO_3$ is used in **Step 1**. At the end of **Step 1** the mass of the CuO is 5.10 g. Calculate the percentage yield of copper oxide.
   Relative atomic masses (A_r): C = 12; O = 16; Cu = 63.5

   Percentage yield = ... %
   [6]

   b) Calculate the percentage atom economy for **Step 2**. Give your answer to two decimal places.

   Atom economy = ... %
   [3]

   c) Another method for obtaining hydrated copper sulfate crystals involves a two-step process:

   Step 1: Add copper carbonate to sulfuric acid until all the acid has reacted.
   $$CuCO_{3(s)} + H_2SO_{4(aq)} \rightarrow CuSO_{4(aq)} + CO_{2(g)} + H_2O_{(l)}$$
   Step 2: Filter the solution then allow it to crystallise.

   The student says the two-step process will give a greater percentage yield than the three-step process. Explain why processes with fewer steps tend to have higher percentage yields.

   ....
   ....
   ....
   [2]

   [Total 11 marks]

Topic 5 — Separate Chemistry 1

2 The Kroll process is an industrial process used to extract titanium from its ore. Some information about the Kroll process and an alternative, theoretical extraction method using electrolysis is shown in **Figure 1**.

Figure 1

Method 1: Kroll Process	**Method 2**: Electrolysis
$TiO_2 + 2Cl_2 + C \rightarrow TiCl_4 + CO_2$ $2Mg + TiCl_4 \rightarrow 2MgCl_2 + Ti$	$TiO_2 \rightarrow Ti + O_2$
Temperatures in the range 700 °C – 1300 °C	Anode temperature 1700 °C
Process can take many days	Slow reaction
Argon atmosphere required	Requires molten salt electrolyte

a) The overall process in **Method 1** can be written as:
$TiO_2 + 2Cl_2 + C + 2Mg \rightarrow CO_2 + 2MgCl_2 + Ti$. Calculate the atom economy for this process.
Give your answer to one decimal place.
Relative formula masses (M_r): $TiO_2 = 80$; $Cl_2 = 71$; $CO_2 = 44$; $MgCl_2 = 95$
Relative atomic masses (A_r): C = 12; Mg = 24; Ti = 48

Atom economy = ... %
[3]

b)* The atom economy of Method 2 is 60%.
Using **Figure 2** and the atom economies of both processes, suggest why titanium is only used for specialised purposes.

....
....
....
....
....
....
....
....
[6]
[Total 9 marks]

Exam Tip
For this last question, the atom economies and table provide all the information you need to get full marks. Review this information from an industrial point of view, thinking about what these factors mean for the production of titanium and why it would only be used for specialised purposes.

Score: 20

Chemical Reactions in Industry

1 The Haber process is used to produce ammonia on an industrial scale.

The equation for the reaction is:

$$N_{2(g)} + 3H_{2(g)} \rightleftharpoons 2NH_{3(g)}$$

The ammonia formed in the reaction is removed by cooling the mixture of gases.
The remaining nitrogen and hydrogen are recycled.

a) State what this suggests about the boiling point of ammonia compared to the other two gases.

....
[1]

Figure 1 shows how temperature and pressure affect the percentage yield of ammonia.

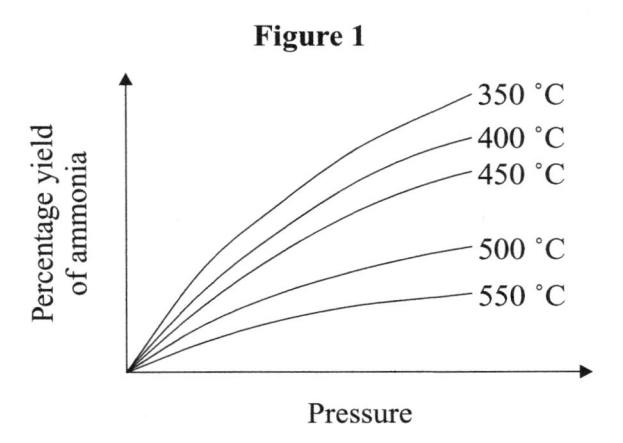

Figure 1

b)* Use the information in **Figure 1** and your own knowledge to explain how the commercially used conditions for the Haber process are related to the yield of ammonia obtained, the cost of the energy used and the rate of reaction.

....
....
....
....
....
....
....
....
[6]
[Total 7 marks]

Topic 5 — Separate Chemistry 1

2 Ammonia can be used to manufacture nitrogen-based fertilisers.
The elements phosphorus and potassium are also important nutrients for plant growth.

a) Write a balanced symbol equation for the reaction between ammonia and nitric acid (HNO$_3$) to form a single product.

....
[1]

b) NPK fertilisers contain the elements nitrogen, phosphorus and potassium in different ratios. They may also contain fillers such as minerals and sand. A label from some fertiliser is shown in **Figure 2**. The number in brackets after the ratio indicates the percentage of the fertiliser that is nitrogen, phosphorus and potassium.

Figure 2

NPK

14 : 11 : 27 (38)

Use the information in **Figure 2** to calculate the masses of nitrogen, phosphorus and potassium present in 500 g of the fertiliser. Give your answers to three significant figures.

Nitrogen: .... g, Phosphorus: .... g, Potassium: .... g
[3]

c) Two methods for producing ammonium nitrate are summarised in **Figure 3**.

Figure 3

Method 1	Method 2
Reaction carried out in giant vats	Reaction carried out by titration
Reactants are very highly concentrated	Reactants have a low concentration
Heat from the reaction used to evaporate off the water from the mixture	Crystallisation used to obtain ammonium nitrate crystals
Product is highly concentrated ammonium nitrate solution	Product is pure ammonium nitrate crystals

Compare the suitability for use in industry of each of these methods.

....
....
....
....
[3]

[Total 7 marks]

Exam Tip

It is a good idea to revise the Haber process specifically (as it often comes up in exams), but you could also be asked about other reversible reactions — watch out for the reversible arrow. Like the Haber process, the equilibrium of these reactions can be shifted by several different factors.

Score: ☐ / 14

Topic 5 — Separate Chemistry 1

Calculations with Gases

1. The equation for the decomposition of hydrogen peroxide is:

$$2H_2O_{2(aq)} \rightarrow 2H_2O_{(l)} + O_{2(g)}$$

a) The decomposition is carried out at room temperature and pressure, using potassium iodide as a catalyst. 60 cm³ of oxygen gas is produced. Calculate the number of moles of oxygen gas produced. The volume of one mole of gas at room temperature and pressure is 24 dm³.

.... mol
[2]

b) The hydrogen peroxide solution contains 60 g of hydrogen peroxide per 1 dm³. Calculate the maximum volume of oxygen gas that could be obtained from 100 cm³ of this solution. Give your answer in dm³ and to two significant figures. The volume of one mole of gas at room temperature and pressure is 24 dm³. Relative formula mass (M_r) of H_2O_2 = 34

Volume = ... dm³
[4]

[Total 6 marks]

2. Solid **A** and Gas **B** are the only two products of a chemical reaction.

200 g of reactants reacted fully to produce 186 g of **A**. Calculate the volume of **B** produced. Give your answer in dm³ to two significant figures. The volume of one mole of gas at room temperature and pressure is 24.0 dm³. Relative formula mass (M_r) of **B** = 44

Volume = ... dm³
[Total 3 marks]

Exam Tip
It's best to get lots of practice with mass, moles and volume formulas. Think each question through carefully to work out how to get to the answer — looking at the units can help you understand what's going on in each step. You will be provided with the standard molar volume if you need it.

Score: ⬜ / 9

Topic 5 — Separate Chemistry 1

Chemical Cells and Fuel Cells

1* **Figure 1** shows some information about two different power sources.

Figure 1

Property	Hydrogen fuel cell	Lithium rechargeable battery
Hazards	Contains hydrogen	Lithium is flammable
Recharging	Requires specialist storage and transfer of hydrogen	Uses standard electrical socket and adapter
Cost per kilowatt hour (p)	10	14
Approximate lifetime (months)	8–12	24–36

Evaluate whether a hydrogen fuel cell or a lithium rechargeable battery would be more suitable for use in a mobile phone. Give reasons for your answer.

....

....

....

....

....

....

....

....

[Total 6 marks]

2 Hydrogen fuel cells are very efficient at generating electricity.

a) Explain why a fuel cell will eventually stop producing a voltage.

....

....
[1]

b) Give **three** reasons why it is unlikely that hydrogen fuel cells will completely replace the use of fossil fuels to generate electricity in the future.

....

....

....
[3]

[Total 4 marks]

> **Exam Tip**
> When a question asks you to evaluate a subject, refer to all the information provided, in enough detail to make it clear you understand it. But don't just repeat the information — you won't get any marks for that. You should also finish with a conclusion based on the points you've made.

Score: /10

Topic 5 — Separate Chemistry 1

Mixed Questions for Paper 1

1 Calcium oxide, CaO, reacts with phosphorus pentoxide, P_4O_{10}, to form a single product, calcium phosphate(V), $Ca_3(PO_4)_2$.

   a) i) Calculate the relative formula mass of calcium phosphate(V).
      Relative atomic masses (A_r): O = 16, P = 31, Ca = 40

      Relative formula mass = ...
      [2]

   ii) Write a balanced equation to show this reaction.

      ....
      [1]

   iii) A sample of solid calcium phosphate(V) is produced by this reaction.
       Explain how you could determine if the sample is contaminated by any reactant.

      ....
      ....
      [2]

   b) Calcium oxide is formed in the decomposition of calcium carbonate.
      In a closed system, this reaction reaches dynamic equilibrium:

      $$CaCO_{3\,(s)} \rightleftharpoons CaO_{(s)} + CO_{2\,(g)}$$

      Explain how the pressure can be changed to increase the yield of calcium oxide.

      ....
      ....
      ....
      [2]
      [Total 7 marks]

2 In a titration, a 25.0 cm³ solution of potassium carbonate, K_2CO_3, is neutralised by 22.5 cm³ of 2.00 mol dm⁻³ sulfuric acid. The equation for the reaction is:

   $$K_2CO_{3\,(aq)} + H_2SO_{4\,(aq)} \rightarrow K_2SO_{4\,(aq)} + H_2O_{(l)} + CO_{2\,(g)}$$

   a) i) Calculate the concentration of the potassium carbonate solution in mol dm⁻³.
      Give your answer to three significant figures.

      Concentration = ... mol dm⁻³
      [4]

ii) A different potassium carbonate solution has a concentration of 2.00 mol dm⁻³.
This solution was made by dissolving some potassium carbonate in 25 cm³ of water.
Calculate the mass of potassium carbonate dissolved in the solution.
Relative atomic masses (A_r): C = 12; O = 16; K = 39

Mass = ... g
[3]

b) The reaction is carried out again, using a solution containing 0.552 g of potassium carbonate and an excess of sulfuric acid, at room temperature and pressure.
Calculate the volume, in dm³, of carbon dioxide gas that is produced.
The volume of one mole of gas at room temperature and pressure is 24.0 dm³.

Volume = ... dm³
[3]

c) i) A student dissolves 5.87 g of potassium carbonate in water to form a solution.
Calculate the volume of 2.00 mol dm⁻³ sulfuric acid required to neutralise this potassium carbonate solution. Give your answer in cm³ and to three significant figures.

Volume = ... cm³
[4]

ii) The student takes a fresh solution of sulfuric acid and adds 20 cm³ of deionised water.
Which of the following will stay the same? Tick **one** box.

☐ **A** The pH of the solution
☐ **B** The concentration of the solution
☐ **C** The strength of the acid
☐ **D** The volume of the solution

[1]

[Total 15 marks]

Mixed Questions for Paper 1

3 A copper sulfate solution was electrolysed using inert graphite electrodes. A deposit of copper metal was formed at the negative electrode. Bubbles were observed at the positive electrode.

a) Suggest the identity of the gas formed at the positive electrode. Explain how this gas is formed.

....

....
[2]

b) Write a balanced half equation to show how this gas is formed.

....
[2]

c) Write a balanced half equation for the reaction that occurs at the cathode.

....
[1]

d) Some potassium chloride solution was added to the copper sulfate solution.
State the products that will now be formed at the anode and cathode. Explain your answers.

....

....

....

....
[4]
[Total 9 marks]

4 Manganese is a transition metal that commonly reacts to form Mn^{2+} ions. A scientist reacts some manganese with dilute sulfuric acid. Neither reactant is in excess. A solution is produced.

a) i) Write a balanced equation for this reaction.

....
[2]

ii) Use your equation to suggest what will be observed in this reaction. Explain your answer.

....

....

....
[3]

b) After the reaction, some iron is added to the product solution. No reaction is observed.
Suggest what would be observed if copper was used instead of iron. Explain your answer.

....

....

....
[2]
[Total 7 marks]

Mixed Questions for Paper 1

40

5   A student is investigating the reactions of Group 2 metals and their compounds.
    The student adds some magnesium to 50 cm³ of 1.0 mol dm⁻³ hydrochloric acid.
    Neither reactant is in excess. The equation for the reaction is:
    $$Mg_{(s)} + 2HCl_{(aq)} \rightarrow MgCl_{2(aq)} + H_{2(g)}$$

a) Calculate the volume of hydrogen produced in this reaction.
   Assume the gas was produced at room temperature and pressure.
   The volume of one mole of any gas at room temperature and pressure is 24.0 dm³.

Volume = ... dm³
[3]

b) Calcium reacts with hydrochloric acid in the same molar ratio as magnesium.
   The student repeated the reaction but replaced the magnesium with the same mass of calcium.
   Predict the effect on the amount of hydrogen produced. Explain your answer.

   ....

   ....

   ....
[3]

c) Calculate the volume of 0.65 mol dm⁻³ Ba(OH)₂ solution required to neutralise 0.020 moles of
   hydrochloric acid. Give your answer in cm³ and to two significant figures.

Volume = ... cm³
[4]

d) The student then reacted magnesium hydroxide, Mg(OH)₂, with hydrochloric acid.
   Magnesium chloride, MgCl₂, was produced with a 60.0% yield.
   Calculate the mass of magnesium hydroxide required to produce 12.5 g of magnesium chloride.
   The molar ratio of Mg(OH)₂ to MgCl₂ in this reaction is 1:1.
   Relative formula masses (M_r): MgCl₂ = 95, Mg(OH)₂ = 58

Mass = ... g
[4]
[Total 14 marks]

Mixed Questions for Paper 1

6 This question is about calcium compounds.

a) Calcium reacts with oxygen to form calcium oxide. Explain why this reaction is a redox reaction.

....

....

[2]

b)* A student wants to make a pure, dry sample of calcium carbonate.
She has access to standard laboratory equipment and the following reagents:
- calcium sulfate powder
- potassium carbonate powder
- calcium chloride powder
- magnesium carbonate powder
- deionised water.

Explain how the student can make a pure, dry sample of calcium carbonate using any of the materials available to her. Include an explanation for any choices you make.

....

....

....

....

....

....

....

....

....

....

....

....

....

....

[6]

[Total 8 marks]

Exam Tip

The questions in your exams won't just stick to one topic, so don't get caught out. Just because a question starts off by asking you about acids doesn't mean the whole of that question will be about acids. You need to be prepared to think across all of the relevant topics for your paper.

Score: ____ / 60

Mixed Questions for Paper 1

Topic 6 — Groups in the Periodic Table

Groups in the Periodic Table

1 This question is about the elements in Group 1 and Group 7 of the periodic table.

a) Predict the structure and bonding of elemental astatine. Explain your prediction.

....

....

[3]

b) Predict the formula of the product that would be formed from the reaction of astatine and potassium. Explain your answer.

....

....

[2]

c) Describe the reaction, if any, that you would expect to take place between astatine and aqueous potassium chloride. Explain your answer.

....

....

[2]

d) Rubidium and iodine are both in Period 5.
Explain why rubidium is highly reactive but iodine has low reactivity.

....

....

....

....

[4]

e)* Compare the reactions with water of lithium and potassium.
Describe what would be observed in each reaction and explain the similarities and differences.

....

....

....

....

....

....

....

....

[6]

[Total 17 marks]

Topic 6 — Groups in the Periodic Table

2 Alkali metals are generally more reactive than other metals.

a) Give **two** other ways in which the typical properties of alkali metals are different from the typical properties of other metals.

....

....

....
[2]

b) Use your knowledge of the electronic configurations of alkali metals to explain how their reactivity changes down the periodic table.

....

....

....

....
[3]
[Total 5 marks]

3 This question is about Group 0 elements.

a) Predict the boiling point of krypton using the data in **Figure 1**.

Figure 1

Element	Boiling point (°C)
neon	−246
argon	−186
xenon	−108

....
[1]

b) Explain why all Group 0 elements are gases at room temperature

....

....

....
[2]

c) In 1962, chemists mixed xenon and fluorine at high pressures. Xenon fluorides were formed. Suggest how this experiment changed the accepted view of Group 0's reactivity. Explain your answer.

....

....

....

....
[3]
[Total 6 marks]

Topic 6 — Groups in the Periodic Table

4 A chemist is investigating the reactions of calcium with chlorine and iodine.

a) Explain, in terms of the electronic structure of the halogens, why the reaction of calcium with chlorine is much faster than the reaction of calcium with iodine.

....

....

....

....
[4]

b) The chemist places a glass lid over a large beaker containing iodine crystals.
She places an ice cube on top of the lid. She then gently heats the bottom of the beaker.
Describe her observations.

....

....

....

....
[4]

[Total 8 marks]

5* Describe what you would expect to observe if you added chlorine water to sodium iodide solution. Explain why the reaction that occurs is a redox reaction. Predict how your observations would differ if you added chlorine water to sodium bromide and sodium chloride instead.

....

....

....

....

....

....

....

....

....

[Total 6 marks]

Exam Tip

If you're stuck on a question about a chemical reaction, try writing out its equation. Seeing it written down might help you work out what's going on — or even get you marks in some questions.

Score: ⬜ / 42

Topic 6 — Groups in the Periodic Table

Topic 7 — Rates of Reaction and Energy Changes

Rates of Reaction

1 The equation for the reaction between sodium thiosulfate solution and dilute hydrochloric acid is:

$$Na_2S_2O_{3(aq)} + 2HCl_{(aq)} \rightarrow 2NaCl_{(aq)} + S_{(s)} + SO_{2(g)} + H_2O_{(l)}$$

Figure 1 shows the experimental setup a student used to investigate the rate of this reaction.

The student recorded the time taken for the cross to become obscured by a precipitate formed during the reaction. He repeated the experiment using five different concentrations of sodium thiosulfate solution.

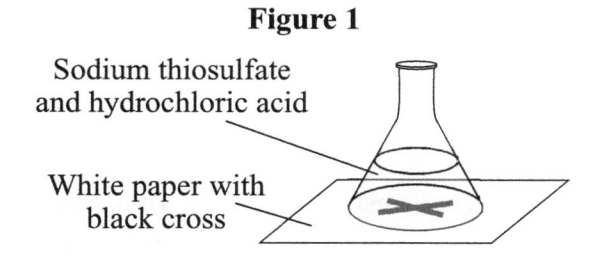

Figure 1

Sodium thiosulfate and hydrochloric acid

White paper with black cross

a) An anomalous result was identified. Which of the following would **not** explain the anomaly? Tick **one** box.

☐ A Using different sized conical flasks for the experiments
☐ B Using different sized measuring cylinders for the reactants
☐ C Adding 20 ml of deionised water to the mixture
☐ D Using a lower concentration of HCl in the final experiment

[1]

The student made different concentrations of sodium thiosulfate solution by diluting $Na_2S_2O_3$ stock solution with water.

Figure 2 shows the student's results. The total volume of stock solution and water was kept constant.

The student concluded that: "Doubling the concentration of $Na_2S_2O_3$ doubles the rate of reaction."

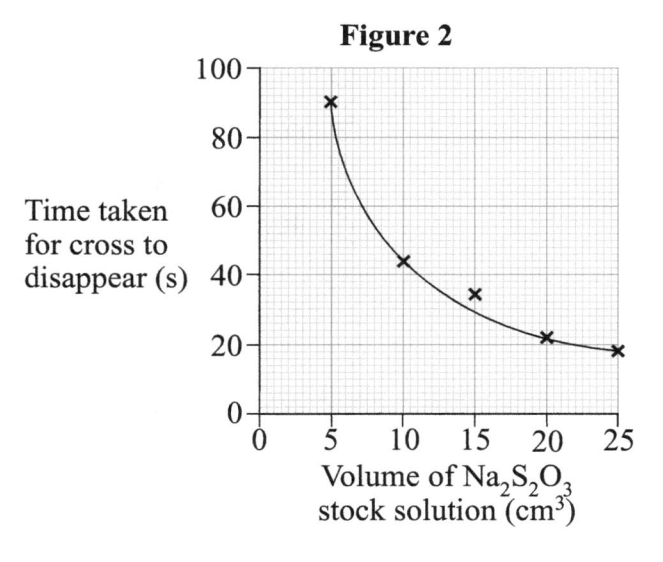

Figure 2

(Graph: Time taken for cross to disappear (s) vs Volume of $Na_2S_2O_3$ stock solution (cm³))

b) What evidence is there to support this conclusion? Use data from **Figure 2** in your answer.

....
....
....
[2]

c) Explain why doubling the concentration doubles the rate of reaction.

....
....
[2]

d) Another student investigated the effect of temperature on the rate of the reaction between sodium thiosulfate and hydrochloric acid. Using your knowledge of collision theory, explain the effect of increasing temperature on reaction rate.

....

....

....

....
[4]

[Total 9 marks]

2 A student investigated the rate of reaction between marble chips and dilute hydrochloric acid. The volume of carbon dioxide gas produced was measured at regular intervals until the reaction was complete.

The results are shown on the graph in **Figure 3**.

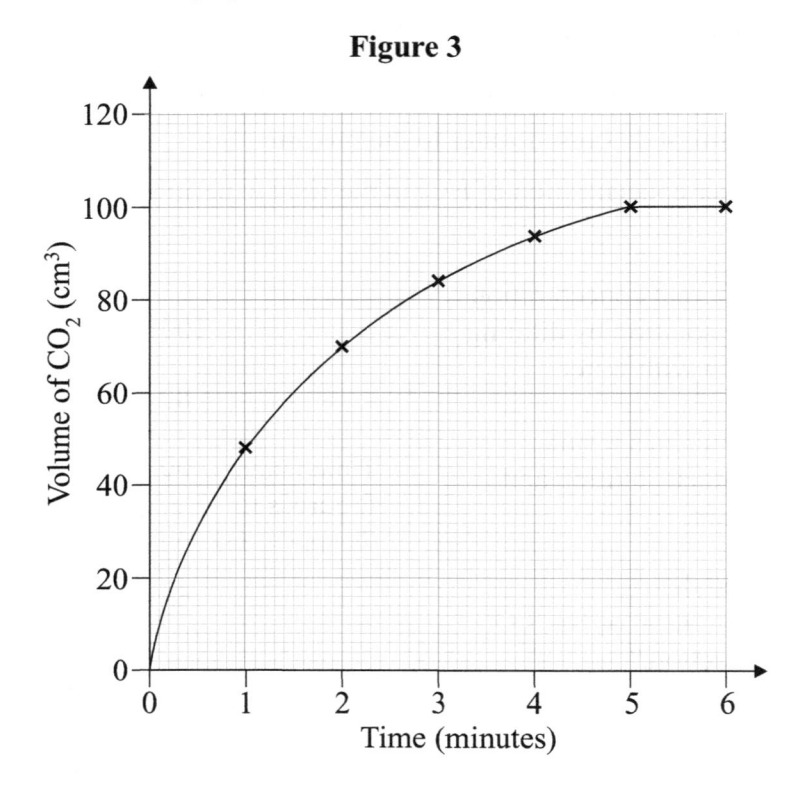

Figure 3

a) Calculate the rate of reaction at 3 minutes. Give your answer to 2 significant figures.

Rate of reaction = ... $cm^3\,min^{-1}$
[3]

b) The student concluded that, "The rate of reaction decreases with time."
Explain how the data in **Figure 3** supports this conclusion.

....

....

....
[2]

Topic 7 — Rates of Reaction and Energy Changes

c) The student repeated the experiment using crushed marble chips. She found that the rate of reaction was too fast to measure the volume of gas accurately. Which of the following changes to the method could she use to decrease the rate of this reaction? Tick **one** box.

- [ ] A Place the conical flask in a bath of ice water
- [ ] B Use a larger volume of hydrochloric acid
- [ ] C Measure the volume of gas every 10 seconds
- [ ] D Use a larger conical flask

[1]
[Total 6 marks]

3 The reaction between magnesium ribbon and excess dilute hydrochloric acid produces hydrogen gas. The rate of reaction was investigated by measuring the mass of the reactants at regular intervals. The results are shown in **Figure 4**.

Figure 4

Time (s)	0	10	20	30	40	50	60
Reactant Mass (g)	103.400	103.374	103.365	103.361	103.359	103.358	103.358

a) On **Figure 5**:
- Plot a graph to show the **loss in mass** against time.
- Draw a line of best fit.

Figure 5

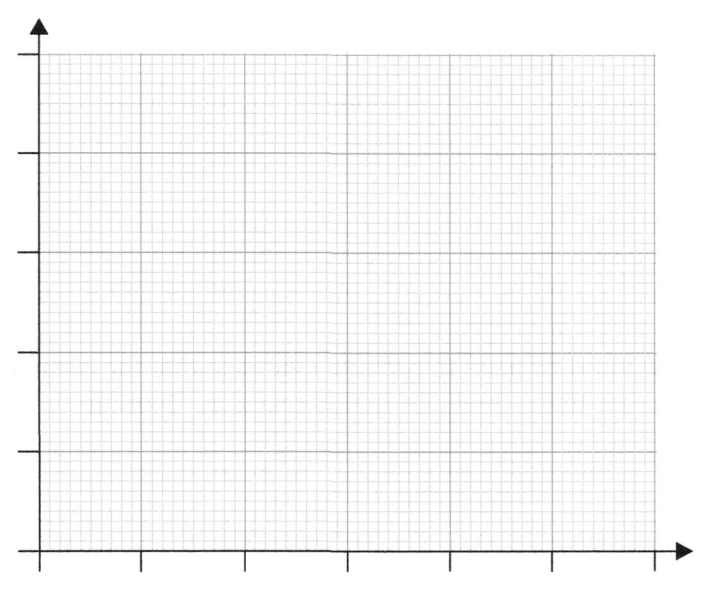

[4]

b) Use your graph to calculate the mean rate of reaction between 15 and 35 seconds.

Mean rate of reaction = ... g s^{-1}
[3]
[Total 7 marks]

Topic 7 — Rates of Reaction and Energy Changes

4 A student investigated the decomposition of dilute hydrogen peroxide using different masses of manganese(IV) oxide catalyst. The student set up the apparatus as shown in **Figure 6**.

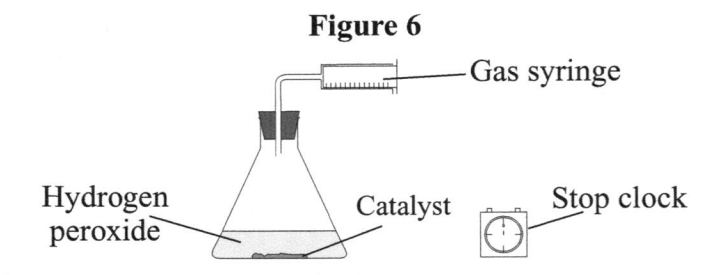

Figure 6 — Gas syringe, Hydrogen peroxide, Catalyst, Stop clock

The student measured masses of powdered catalyst between 0.1 g and 0.7 g and placed each into a conical flask containing 15 cm³ of hydrogen peroxide solution. The student recorded the volume of gas produced in 60 seconds for each mass of catalyst.

a) Explain why a greater volume of gas was collected when using a greater mass of catalyst.

....
[1]

b)* Another student repeated the experiment, using the same masses of powdered catalyst, but recorded the volume of gas produced every 10 seconds over the course of one minute.

Compare the methods used by the two students, and explain how the second method could provide more evidence to support a conclusion about the effect of catalyst mass on the rate of reaction.

....
....
....
....
....
....
....
....
[6]

c) Describe a method that could be used to provide evidence that the manganese(IV) oxide behaved as a catalyst rather than a reactant in this reaction. Explain your answer.

....
....
....
....
[3]

[Total 10 marks]

Exam Tip
To calculate the rate of reaction at a certain point in time from a graph, you need to draw a tangent to the curve. The mark scheme will accept answers within a range, but it's important to draw the tangent carefully — adjust your ruler so the space between it and the curve is equal on both sides.

Score: ☐ / 32

Topic 7 — Rates of Reaction and Energy Changes

Energy Changes

1 A student is investigating the temperature change of the reaction between sodium carbonate and citric acid. The results of the experiment are shown in **Figure 1**.

This is the method used:
1. Place 25 cm³ of sodium carbonate solution in a polystyrene cup.
2. Measure the temperature of the solution.
3. Add 1.2 g of citric acid, and stir the solution.
4. Place a lid on the cup.
5. When the reaction is complete, measure the temperature of the final solution.
6. Repeat the experiment three times, and calculate the mean temperature change.
7. Repeat the experiment, keeping all variables the same, except for the mass of citric acid.

Figure 1

Mass of citric acid added (g)	Mean temperature change (°C)
1.2	−0.3
3.2	−0.9
6.0	−1.4
7.5	−2.0
10.0	−2.5

a) On **Figure 2**:
- Plot these results on the grid.
- Draw a line of best fit.

Figure 2

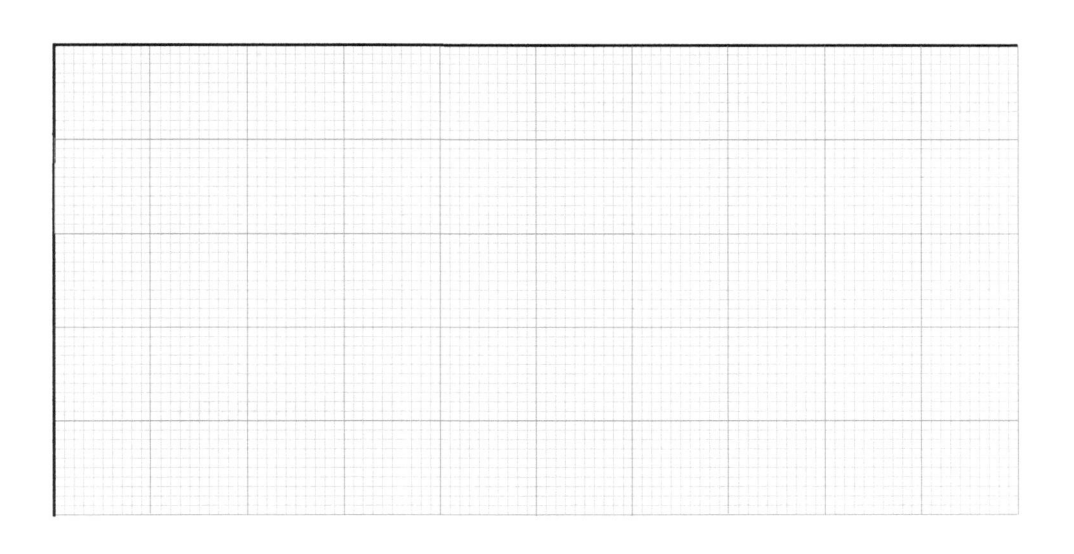

Mass of citric acid added (g)

[3]

b) Predict the temperature change that would occur if 5 g of citric acid was added to the sodium carbonate solution.

....

[1]

Topic 7 — Rates of Reaction and Energy Changes

c) Give **one** thing the student has done to increase the accuracy of the results. Explain your answer.

....

....

....
[2]

d) A scientist makes the following statement:

"The reaction of carbonate ions with acid is an endothermic reaction that occurs at room temperature."

Explain this statement in terms of bonds and activation energy.

....

....

....
[2]

[Total 8 marks]

2 Nitrogen and hydrogen react together in the following way: $N_2 + 3H_2 \rightarrow 2NH_3$.

The overall energy change of the reaction is –97 kJ mol⁻¹. The N≡N bond energy is 941 kJ mol⁻¹ and the N–H bond energy is 391 kJ mol⁻¹. The displayed formula of NH_3 is shown in **Figure 3**.

Figure 3

Calculate the energy of the H–H bond.

H–H bond energy = ... kJ mol⁻¹

[Total 4 marks]

Exam Tip

When dealing with energy change questions, pay close attention to the number of bonds and the number of molecules involved in the reaction. Also, be careful with positive and negative numbers if you have to rearrange the equation. The best thing to do is practice these questions plenty of times.

Score: ☐ / 12

Topic 7 — Rates of Reaction and Energy Changes

Topic 8 — Fuels and Earth Science

Fuels

1 Hydrocarbon **A** is a hydrocarbon molecule containing 10 carbon atoms.

Figure 1 represents a two-step process that is used to produce poly(ethene) from Hydrocarbon **A**. When its hot vapours are passed over a heated catalyst, hydrocarbons **B** and **C** are formed in a 1:1 ratio. Poly(ethene) is produced by addition polymerisation of Hydrocarbon **C**.

Figure 1

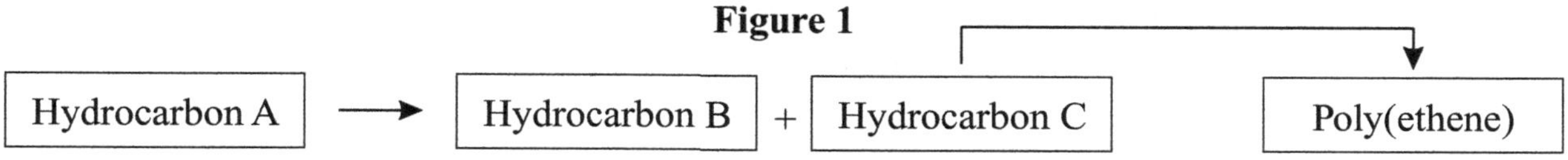

Hydrocarbon A ⟶ Hydrocarbon B + Hydrocarbon C ⟶ Poly(ethene)

a) Give the formulas of hydrocarbons **A**, **B** and **C**.

Hydrocarbon A ....   Hydrocarbon B: ....   Hydrocarbon C: ....
[3]

b)* Compare the properties of hydrocarbon **A** with those of the hydrocarbon $C_{35}H_{72}$.
Explain why hydrocarbon **A** might be a more desirable product than $C_{35}H_{72}$.

....
....
....
....
....
....
....
....
....
[6]

c) Other reactions can occur when hot vapours of hydrocarbon **A** are passed over a heated catalyst. Write an equation to show hydrocarbon **C** and one other product being formed in the ratio 3:1.

....
[1]

[Total 10 marks]

2 Nitrogen monoxide is a gas formed in vehicle engines.

When released, nitrogen monoxide can combine with oxygen in the air to form nitrogen dioxide. Nitrogen dioxide reacts with more oxygen and water in the air to form nitric acid (HNO_3). Give balanced equations for both the formation of nitrogen dioxide from nitrogen monoxide, **and** the formation of nitric acid from nitrogen dioxide.

1. ....

2. ....

[Total 2 marks]

3 Burning fossil fuels for transportation contributes to the level of carbon dioxide in the atmosphere.

a) Petrol contains the hydrocarbon octane (C_8H_{18}).
Write a balanced symbol equation for the combustion of octane in an excess of oxygen.

....
[2]

b) Solid particles of carbon, known as soot, can be formed when octane combusts in a limited supply of oxygen. Various other products may also be produced. Write a possible balanced symbol equation to show this.

....
[2]

c) Describe how the products of incomplete combustion impact human health.

....

....

....

....

....
[3]

[Total 7 marks]

4 Fractional distillation separates crude oil into mixtures containing hydrocarbons of similar length. The diesel fraction of crude oil contains $C_{16}H_{34}$ molecules.

Some of these molecules are cracked for economic reasons. Explain this statement.

....

....

....

....

....

....

[Total 4 marks]

Exam Tip
Pay close attention to any information you're given in the question — if it helps, you could even underline the important bits so that you can refer back to them quickly. You'll often need to apply your own knowledge to some information you're given in order to work something out.

Score: ☐ / 23

Topic 8 — Fuels and Earth Science

Earth and Atmospheric Science

1   The level of carbon dioxide in the atmosphere at the South Pole every ten years between 1960 and 2010 is shown in **Figure 1**. The values have been rounded to the nearest 5 parts per million.

Figure 1

Year	1960	1970	1980	1990	2000	2010
CO_2 (parts per million)	315	325	335	350	365	385

a)* Describe the trend in carbon dioxide levels shown in **Figure 1**. Suggest the effects of this trend on the global average surface temperature and the global mean sea level. Explain your answers.

....

....

....

....

....

....

....

....

[6]

Figure 2 shows some data about historic levels of carbon dioxide in the atmosphere.

Figure 2

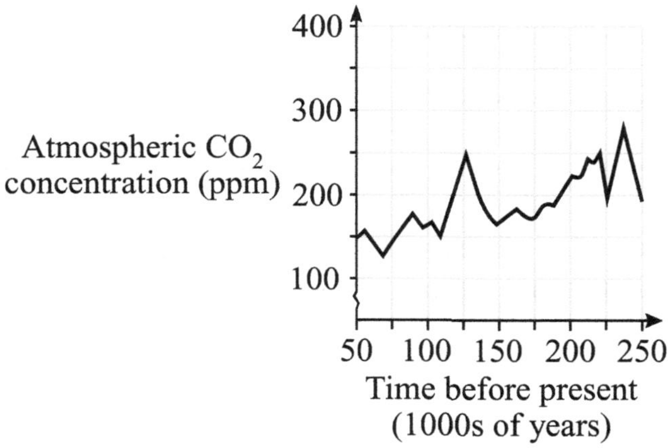

b) Suggest **two** reasons why the data in **Figure 2** might not be as reliable as current global data.

1. ....

....

2. ....

....

[2]

[Total 8 marks]

Topic 8 — Fuels and Earth Science

2   Earth's early atmosphere is thought to have been similar to the atmosphere of Venus today. The percentage compositions of the modern-day atmospheres of Earth and Venus are shown in **Figure 3**.

Figure 3

Percentage composition of atmosphere (%)	Nitrogen	Oxygen	Argon	Carbon dioxide	Water vapour
Earth today	78	21	0.93	0.036	0-4.0
Venus today	3.5	trace	trace	96.5	trace

a) Explain the difference in oxygen levels between Earth's early atmosphere and Earth's atmosphere today.

....

....

....

....

....

[3]

b) Venus has the highest average surface temperature of any planet in the Solar System. Use the data in **Figure 3** to suggest why Venus is so much hotter than Earth today.

....

....

....

....

....

[3]

c) Changes in today's atmosphere are taking place as a result of human activities. Give the name of **one** of these activities and the gas it produces.

....

....

[2]

[Total 8 marks]

Exam Tip

When you're given a table as part of a question, take a good look at it to make sure you understand what it shows. It could show how one variable changes over time (as in Figure 1) or show multiple variables (as in Figure 3). Make sure you pick out only the data that's relevant to the question and clearly explain how it supports your answer.

Topic 8 — Fuels and Earth Science

Target AO3

3* **Figure 4** shows a section from a news report about the effects of global climate change on a country.

Figure 4

> Country X is considered to be one of the countries that is most at risk from the effects of climate change. Large parts of the country, particularly in the south, are low-lying and could be seriously affected by increasing global temperatures and rising sea levels.
>
> An international committee of scientists conducted a peer-reviewed study over 50 years, in which the temperature was measured twice a year at ten separate locations across Country X. Data from the study has shown that the average annual temperature for Country X has increased by around 0.5 °C since 1970. Furthermore, the scientists have predicted that there will be a 3-4 °C increase in the average annual temperature by the end of the century if global greenhouse gas emissions continue to increase at the current rate.
>
> However, a regional oil company has disputed the findings. The company carried out their own study by measuring the temperature at their headquarters in the north of Country X annually for 10 years. Results from their study show that the temperature has risen by 0.1 °C in that time. A spokesperson for the company stated, "Our data shows there is no significant change to average annual temperature, despite the increase in greenhouse gas levels. We believe that this suggests that greenhouse gas emissions are not affecting the climate as some scientists have suggested."

Use the information given in the report to evaluate the two studies, and suggest which study is more useful when considering the possible effects of climate change on Country X.

....
....
....
....
....
....
....
....
....
....
....

[Total 6 marks]

Score:

22

Topic 8 — Fuels and Earth Science

Topic 9 — Separate Chemistry 2

Tests for Ions

1* A student is given four reagent bottles labelled A, B, C and D, each containing a powdered solid. The student is told that the bottles contain the soluble salts sodium bromide, potassium carbonate, sodium sulfate and potassium chloride.

The student is given access to the following:

- A loop of nichrome metal
- Deionised water
- Dilute nitric acid
- Dilute hydrochloric acid
- Silver nitrate solution
- Barium chloride solution
- A Bunsen burner

Devise a step-by-step method that the student could use to confirm **both** the cation and the anion present in each of the bottles.
Include the expected results of each test and explain what they show.

....
....
....
....
....
....
....
....
....
....

[Total 6 marks]

2 **Figure 1** shows the results of some chemical tests to identify two compounds.

Figure 1

Compound	A	$CaCl_2$
Flame Test	Crimson	B ....
Add excess NaOH solution	No visible change	C ....
Add dilute HNO_3	No visible change	D ....
Add dilute HNO_3 and $AgNO_3$ solution	Yellow precipitate	E ....

a) Use your knowledge of the results of chemical tests to fill in boxes **A** to **E** in **Figure 1**.

[5]

Topic 9 — Separate Chemistry 2

b) Write a balanced ionic equation for the reaction between calcium chloride and sodium hydroxide solution. Include state symbols.

....

[2]
[Total 7 marks]

3 The flame emission spectrum for a sample of an unknown substance is shown in **Figure 2**. The flame emission spectra for four elements possibly contained in the sample are also shown.

Figure 2

a) Use the spectra provided to determine which element could **not** be present in the sample.

....

[1]

b) The spectral lines below 400 nm and at 550 nm were observed to be brighter than the others. Use the data from the spectra to explain what this suggests about the composition of the sample.

....

....

....

[2]
[Total 3 marks]

Exam Tip
The results for ion tests are something you've just got to remember, but there are a couple of patterns that might help. As you go down the periodic table, the halides (chloride, bromide, iodide) produce a yellower precipitate with silver nitrate. See if you can spot any of your own patterns.

Score: / 16

Topic 9 — Separate Chemistry 2

Reactions of Organic Compounds

1   A student is studying organic compounds. He draws the four structures shown in **Figure 1**.

Figure 1

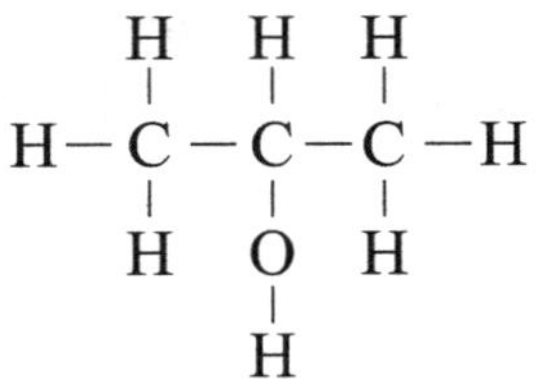

A, 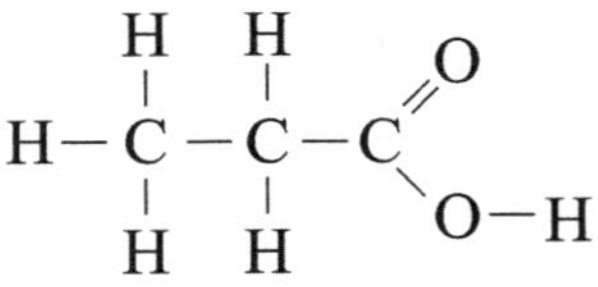 B, 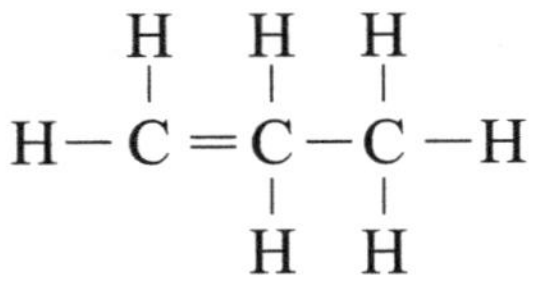 C, 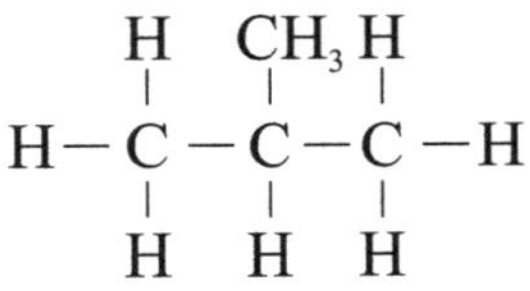 D structures shown.

a) Which of the four structures in **Figure 1** has been drawn incorrectly? Tick **one** box.

☐ A   ☐ B   ☐ C   ☐ D

[1]

The student was asked to draw the structure of butene.
The student drew the structure shown in **Figure 2**.

Figure 2

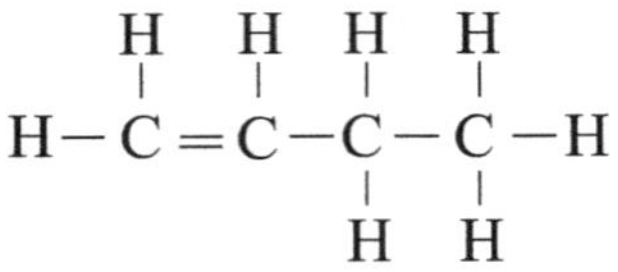

b) Draw an alternative structure for butene. Explain why the structure you have drawn is also correct.

....

....
[2]

c) Butanoic acid can be produced from butene by first converting it into an alcohol.
   Name the alcohol and give the chemical formulas of the alcohol and butanoic acid.

....

....
[3]

d) Alkenes react with bromine water. During the reaction, the bromine water loses its orange colour. Describe the change in the structure of the alkene and explain this observation.

....

....

....

....
[3]

[Total 9 marks]

2 Glycolic acid (CH₂OHCOOH) is a solid at room temperature. It is a weak acid used as an ingredient in chemical face peels. Its structure is shown in **Figure 3**.

Figure 3

a) Suggest why glycolic acid undergoes reactions of **both** carboxylic acids and alcohols.

....

....
[1]

b) Describe what is observed when glycolic acid reacts with sodium carbonate solution (Na₂CO₃). Explain your answer. Include a balanced equation with state symbols.

....

....

....

....

....
[4]

c) Describe what happens to the structure of glycolic acid when it reacts with an oxidizing agent. Include a drawing of the structure of the compound produced.

....

....
[2]

[Total 7 marks]

Exam Tip
You'll be expected to know the prefixes meth-, eth-, prop- and but- in the exam, but you might also come across larger compounds or ones with special names. Unless told otherwise, assume that these have the same properties and undergo the same reactions as the ones you're familiar with.

Score: ☐ / 16

Topic 9 — Separate Chemistry 2

Polymers

1 Polymers are used for a wide variety of purposes.

a) PCTFE is an addition polymer formed from chlorotrifluoroethene.
Figure 1 shows the structure of chlorotrifluoroethene.
Draw a diagram to represent the formation of PCTFE from chlorotrifluoroethene.

Figure 1

$$\begin{array}{c} F \quad F \\ | \quad | \\ C = C \\ | \quad | \\ F \quad Cl \end{array}$$

[2]

b) The two monomers shown in **Figure 2** undergo a polymerisation reaction.

Figure 2

$$\begin{array}{c} H \quad H \\ | \quad | \\ HO - C - C - OH \\ | \quad | \\ H \quad H \end{array} \qquad \begin{array}{c} O \quad H \quad H \quad H \quad H \quad H \quad H \quad O \\ \| \quad | \quad | \quad | \quad | \quad | \quad | \quad \| \\ HO - C - C - C - C - C - C - C - C - OH \\ \quad | \quad | \quad | \quad | \quad | \quad | \\ \quad H \quad H \quad H \quad H \quad H \quad H \end{array}$$

Name the type of polymerisation reaction that occurs. Describe what happens during the reaction.

Name: ....

Description: ....

....
[3]

c)* Describe the problems associated with producing and disposing of plastic polymers and suggest an explanation for why plastic polymers are still widely used despite these problems.

....

....

....

....

....

....

....

....

[6]
[Total 11 marks]

Exam Tip
For questions like Q1c, give a good amount of detail about each factor involved, explaining why each of them is good or bad and what/who for. Remember to include a sentence or two on anything the question asks for specifically — if you don't, it's a really easy way to lose out on marks.

Score: / 11

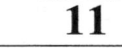

Topic 9 — Separate Chemistry 2

Nanoparticles

1 A block of gold, Cube **A**, has a side length of 12 nm.

a) Explain whether Cube **A** would be classed as a nanoparticle.

....

....
[1]

b) Calculate the surface area to volume ratio of Cube **A**.

Surface area to volume ratio = ...
[3]

c) Cube **A** is cut to make 8 equal sized cubes.
What is the total surface area to volume ratio of these eight cubes?

Surface area to volume ratio = ...
[2]

d) Cube **B** has a side length that is 3 times smaller than the original side length of Cube **A**.
What is the surface area to volume ratio of Cube **B**?
Tick **one** box.

☐ **A** 2 : 3
☐ **B** 3 : 6
☐ **C** 1 : 6
☐ **D** 3 : 2

[1]
[Total 7 marks]

Topic 9 — Separate Chemistry 2

2 A scientist is investigating a new way of administering drugs by bonding them to the surface of nanoparticles.

a) Explain how decreasing the size of each nanoparticle affects the amount of drug bonded per gram of nanoparticles.

....

....
[2]

The scientist makes two sizes of nanoparticle.
Nanoparticle **A** has a diameter of 100 nm. Nanoparticle **B** has a diameter of 25 nm.

b) Nanoparticle **A** is approximated to a cube with edges of 100 nm and its surface area to volume ratio is calculated. Which of the following is the best estimate of this ratio? Tick **one** box.

☐ A 3 : 50
☐ B 50 : 3
☐ C 3 : 5
☐ D 30 : 5
[1]

c) The quantity of drug molecules that can be attached to these nanoparticles is directly proportional to their surface area. By approximating to a cube, calculate the surface area to volume ratio of Nanoparticle **B**. Use your answer to compare the quantity of drug molecules that can be attached per unit volume of Nanoparticles **A** and **B**.

....

....

....

....

....
[4]

d) The scientist heated a sample of each type of nanoparticle. Both samples were found to melt at a very different temperature to that which other substances with similar molar masses melt at. Suggest an explanation of why the particle model may be of limited use in understanding the properties of the nanoparticles.

....

....
[1]

[Total 8 marks]

Exam Tip

To get the top grades, it's a good idea to attempt every question on the paper, so you can pick up as many marks as possible. If you're not sure about a multiple choice question like 2b), start off by trying to rule out any obviously wrong answers. You can then use the remaining answers to make an educated guess.

Topic 9 — Separate Chemistry 2

Target AO3

3 Figure 1 contains a selection of properties of silver nanoparticles.

a) Research is being carried out into the use of silver nanoparticles as an ingredient in some skin products. Use your existing knowledge and the properties given in **Figure 1** to evaluate the use of silver nanoparticles in skin products.

Figure 1

Properties of Silver Nanoparticles
Can catalyse a range of reactions.
Able to kill a range of microorganisms.
Soluble in water.
Can release toxic ions when dissolved.

....

[4]

b) Silver nanoparticles can also be used in water treatment processes. A scientist wants to compare how effective two different processes are. Process **A** is a standard water treatment process. Process **B** is identical but also uses silver nanoparticles. Here is the method that the scientist uses:

1. Collect six samples of untreated water from the same source.
2. Treat three samples using process **A**, and treat the other three samples using process **B**.
3. Analyse each treated water sample and calculate a mean value for the cleanliness of the water samples treated with process **A**, and a mean value for those treated with process **B**.
4. Compare the mean values for water cleanliness for each process.

i) Explain one thing that the scientist has done in order to increase the accuracy of the results.

....

[2]

ii) Give one way in which the scientist could have increased the accuracy of the results further.

....

[1]

[Total 7 marks]

Score:

22

Topic 9 — Separate Chemistry 2

Properties of Materials

1 Carbon fibre is a material made from carbon atoms embedded in a polymer matrix. Carbon fibre is very strong and lightweight, and is used in sports car manufacturing.

a) What type of material is carbon fibre?

....
[1]

b) Suggest a reason why low carbon steel is more often used to make the bodies of family cars, despite carbon fibre being much stronger and more lightweight.

....
[1]

c) Aluminium alloys are stronger and more lightweight than low carbon steel. Give **one** other reason why aluminium alloys might be a more suitable material for car bodies than low carbon steel.

....
[1]

[Total 3 marks]

2* A plumbing company is developing new piping for hot water.
Information about two polymers the company could use is given in **Figure 1**.

Figure 1

Property	Polymer A	Polymer B
Cost per kg (£)	0.5	5
Average chain length	200	225
Response to heating to 100 °C	Softens	No change
Response to heating to 500 °C	Burns with a smoky flame	Chars
Response to stretching	Thins and eventually breaks	Resists stretching
Chemical reactivity	Inert to water, acids and alkalis	Inert to water, acids and alkalis
Density (g cm^{-3})	0.5	2.0

Use **Figure 1** to evaluate how suitable each polymer is for the piping.
State which polymer is the best material for the company to use. Explain your answer.

....

....

....

....

....

....

....

[Total 6 marks]

Topic 9 — Separate Chemistry 2

3 This question is about alloys.

a) The main body of an aircraft is made of an alloy of aluminium that contains 4.5% copper, 0.6% manganese, 1.5% magnesium and 0.5% other elements. The total mass is 68 500 kg. Calculate the mass of aluminium it contains. Give your answer to three significant figures.

Mass = ... kg
[2]

Figure 2 shows how the tensile strength of an alloy changes with the percentage of copper it contains.

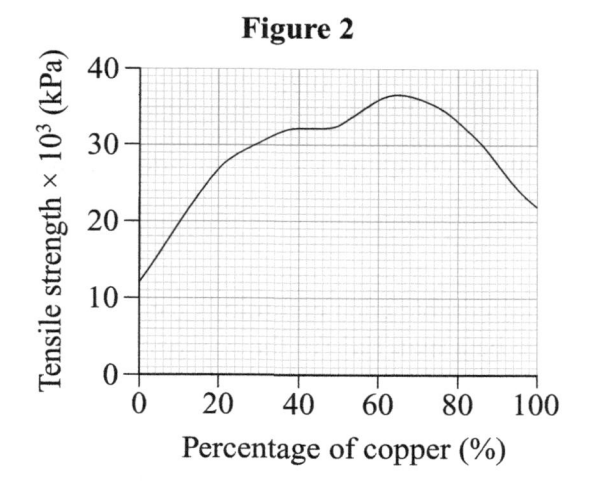

Figure 2

b) A student said, "The higher the percentage of copper in the alloy, the greater the tensile strength of the alloy." Use the graph to explain whether or not the student was correct.

....

....

....
[2]

c) Use **Figure 2** to calculate the difference in tensile strength between pure copper and the alloy containing 8% copper.

.... kPa
[2]
[Total 6 marks]

Exam Tip

It's important that you feel confident using graphs to help you answer questions in the exam. As well as interpreting what the graph is showing you, you could be asked to plot data, to draw lines from the axes to obtain information, to find the slope of a linear graph and where it intercepts the vertical axis, or to find the tangent to a curve.

Topic 9 — Separate Chemistry 2

Target AO3

4   A kitchenware company is producing some new dinner plates.
Information about three ceramics the company could use is given in **Figure 3**.

Fracture toughness is a measure of how likely a material is to crack.
Materials with a lower fracture toughness are more likely to crack under stress.

Figure 3

Property	Ceramic A	Ceramic B	Ceramic C
Density (kg m^{-3})	2400	2400	4000
Compressive strength (MPa)	20	500	2100
Tensile strength (MPa)	4	130	250
Fracture toughness (MPa m$^{1/2}$)	0.75	2	4.4

a) Suggest another property that the company should consider when choosing their material.

....
[1]

b)* Use **Figure 3** to evaluate how suitable each ceramic is for making dinner plates.
Suggest which ceramic is the best material for the company to use.

....
....
....
....
....
....
....
....
[6]

c) Ceramic **C** is a form of alumina (aluminium oxide, Al$_2$O$_3$).
Alumina is commonly used to make joint replacements as it is chemically inert.
Use this information and the data in **Figure 3** to suggest
why alumina is a suitable material for this purpose.

....
....
....
....
[2]

[Total 9 marks]

Topic 9 — Separate Chemistry 2

Target AO3

5 A tensile test machine is a piece of equipment used to test tensile strength. Two ends of a sample of material are gripped by the machine. The machine pulls each end and records the amount of force required to break the sample, as well as how far it stretches before breaking.

a) **Figure 4** shows the tensile strengths of three metals, **A**, **B** and **C**. One metal is pure copper, one is cupronickel (an alloy of copper and nickel), and one is brass (an alloy of copper and zinc).

Figure 4

Metal	Tensile strength (MPa)
A	350
B	210
C	360

Suggest which of the three metals shown in **Figure 4** is pure copper. Explain your answer.

....
....
....
....

[3]

b) **Figure 5** shows the tensile strength of pure nickel and of nichrome. Nichrome is an alloy of nickel and chromium.

Figure 5

Metal	Tensile strength (MPa)
Nickel	390
Nichrome	715

i) A student concluded, "The data shows that the more chromium there is in any metal alloy, the higher its tensile strength will be."
Give and explain one piece of evidence from the table that supports the student's statement.

....
....
....

[2]

ii) Give and explain one reason why the student's conclusion might not be correct.

....
....
....

[2]

[Total 7 marks]

Score: ⬜

31

Topic 9 — Separate Chemistry 2

Mixed Questions for Paper 2

1   A student carried out a series of reactions to investigate the reactivity of two unknown elements, **A** and **Z**. His results are shown in **Figure 1**.

Figure 1

Reaction	Results
A with aqueous potassium iodide	Forms a brown solution containing a covalent compound and an ionic compound. An aqueous solution of this ionic compound reacts with Cl_2 to produce an orange solution.
A with **Z**	Forms a white solid that dissolves in water.
Z with water	Vigorous reaction to form a metal hydroxide solution with a pH of 12. The metal hydroxide contains 69.64% **Z** by mass.

a) Identify element **A**. Explain your reasoning.

A = ...

Reasoning: ....

....

....

....

....

[4]

b) Identify element **Z**. Explain your reasoning. Include any relevant calculations.

Z = ...

Reasoning: ....

....

....

....

....

....

[4]

c) In another experiment, the student adds an excess of chlorine to aqueous lithium iodide. The solution turns brown. The student then adds a few drops of acidified silver nitrate solution to the brown solution. Suggest what you would expect the student to observe. Explain your answer.

....

....

....

[3]

[Total 11 marks]

2 Carbon fullerenes are a type of nanoparticle.

a) Suggest, in terms of its structure, why buckminsterfullerene (C₆₀) could potentially be used in medicine to deliver drugs directly to specific cells.

....
....
....
....
....
[4]

b) Suggest **one** reason why this technique might result in medical side effects.

....
....
[1]

Figure 2 shows the structure of a carbon nanotube.

Figure 2

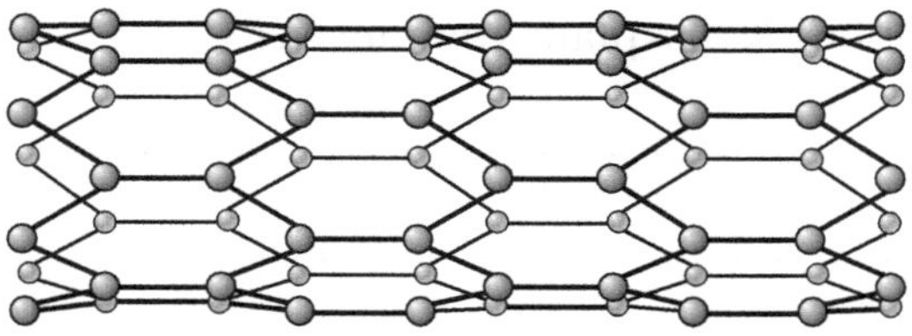

c) Using **Figure 2** and your own knowledge, suggest an explanation of why carbon nanotubes are strong materials.

....
....
....
[2]

d) Use **Figure 2** to explain why carbon nanotubes have high electrical conductivity.

....
....
....
[2]

e) Suggest an explanation of why carbon nanotubes are used in catalyst systems.

....
....
....
[3]

[Total 12 marks]

3 A student is investigating how efficient various alcohols are when used as fuels.

First, she measures the mass of propanol required to increase the temperature of a sample of water by 25 °C. Her apparatus is shown in **Figure 3**.

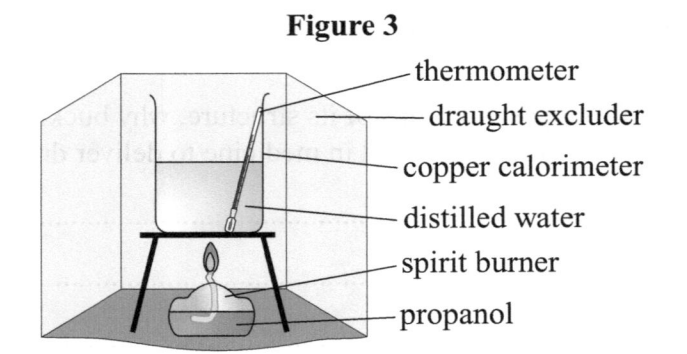

Figure 3
- thermometer
- draught excluder
- copper calorimeter
- distilled water
- spirit burner
- propanol

a) Suggest **one** change that the student could make to the set-up of her apparatus in order to make the result more accurate. Explain your answer.

....

....

....
[2]

b) The student finds that 0.49 g of propanol is needed to raise the temperature of the water by 25 °C. The student repeats the experiment using a different alcohol, **X**. 0.60 g of **X** is required to raise the temperature of the water by 25 °C.

Suggest the identity of alcohol **X**. Explain your answer.

....

....

....

....
[4]

c) The reaction profile for the combustion of 0.49 g of propanol is shown in **Figure 4**.

Explain how **Figure 4** shows that the combustion of propanol is exothermic.

Figure 4

(Energy vs Progress of reacton; Reactants higher than Products)

....

....

....
[1]

d) Describe how the reaction profile for the combustion of 0.49 g of pentanol would differ from **Figure 4**. Explain your answer.

....

....

....

....
[3]

Mixed Questions for Paper 2

e)* Describe a method for producing ethanol by fermentation. Explain any necessary conditions.

....

....

....

....

....

....

....

....

....

[6]
[Total 16 marks]

4 This question is about bonding in hydrocarbons.

Figure 5

a) Ethane has the formula C_2H_6.
   Figure 5 shows the outer shells of the atoms in ethane.

   Label **Figure 5** with the correct symbol for each atom, and turn it into a dot and cross diagram by showing the arrangement of the outer shell electrons.
   Use dots to represent the electrons on the carbon atoms, and use crosses to represent the electrons on the hydrogen atoms.

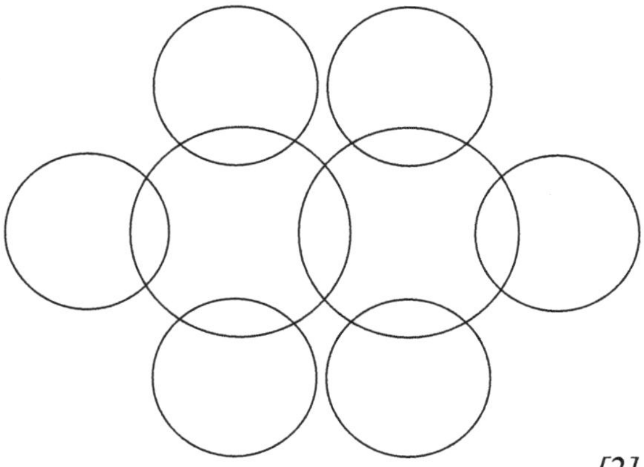

   [2]

b) Ethene has the formula C_2H_4. In terms of electronic structure, explain why there is a double covalent bond between the two carbon atoms.

....

....

....

....

[4]

c) A student makes the following statement:
   "The C=C double bond in ethene is stronger than the C–C single bond in ethane. This means that ethene will have a higher boiling point than ethane." Evaluate the student's statement.

....

....

....

[2]
[Total 8 marks]

Mixed Questions for Paper 2

5   This question is about iron and its compounds.

a) Iron and oxygen react to form an ionic compound, iron(III) oxide, Fe_2O_3. This is the only product.

i) Explain why iron can be rolled into flat sheets, but iron oxide cannot.

....

....

....

....
[4]

ii) Calculate the mass of Fe_2O_3 ($M_r = 160$) that contains 4.50×10^{24} iron(III) ions.

mass = ... g
[3]

b) i) Describe how the presence of iron(II) ions in a solution could be determined chemically. Name the compound that would form during the chemical test.

....

....

....
[3]

ii) Write a balanced ionic equation for the reaction you described above. Include state symbols.

....
[3]

c) A solution containing iron ions is thought to be contaminated with other metal ions. The solution is analysed using flame emission spectroscopy. **Figure 6** shows the wavelengths (in 10^{-10} m) of some of the lines in the spectrum of the metal ion solution, and in the spectra of some reference solutions that contain only one metal.

Figure 6

Metal solution	Fe solution	Mn solution	V solution	Zn solution
4041	4144	4041	4112	4722
4144	5167	4783	4379	4811
4783	6456	6022	4408	6362
5167				
6022				
6456				

Suggest the identity of the other metal present in the solution.
Explain your answer using data from **Figure 6**.

....

....
[2]

[Total 15 marks]

6 One mole of sulfur dioxide will react with one mole of water and half a mole of oxygen gas to form one mole of sulfuric acid:
$$SO_2 + H_2O + 0.5O_2 \rightarrow H_2SO_4$$

a) Explain how sulfur dioxide in the atmosphere can have a negative impact on aquatic species.

....

....
[2]

The structures of SO_2 and H_2SO_4 are given in **Figure 7**.
The bond energies are shown in **Figure 8**.

Figure 7

Figure 8

Bond	Energy (kJ mol⁻¹)
S = O	522
O = O	494
O – H	459
S – O	265

b) i) Calculate the overall energy change of this reaction.

energy change = ... kJ mol⁻¹
[3]

ii) If there is no oxygen present, sulfur dioxide will react with water to produce sulfurous acid, H_2SO_3: $SO_2 + H_2O \rightarrow H_2SO_3$
The structure of sulfurous acid is shown in **Figure 9**.
Use your answer to part **i)** to find the overall energy change for this reaction. A full energy change calculation is not required.

Figure 9

[3]
[Total 8 marks]

Exam Tip
In an exam it can be easy to rush and hit the wrong button on your calculator without realising. Do calculations a couple of times to check that you haven't made any silly mistakes. Use your common sense, too — if your answer doesn't seem realistic in relation to the question, try it again.

Score: ☐ / 70

Mixed Questions for Paper 2

Answers

Topic 1 — Key Concepts in Chemistry

Pages 1-2 — Atomic Structure and the Periodic Table

1 a) Relative atomic mass (A_r)
= (sum of (isotope abundance × isotope mass number))
÷ sum of abundances of all the isotopes
= ((7.5 × 6) + (92.5 × 7)) ÷ (7.5 + 92.5)
= 692.5 ÷ 100 = 6.925 = **6.9** to 1 d.p.
[3 marks for the correct answer, otherwise 1 mark for reading correct values from y-axis and 1 mark for correct calculation]
Name = lithium *[1 mark]*

b) X = Li, which has 3 electrons. In LiCl, Li exists as the ion Li⁺, which has 3 − 1 = 2 electrons.
So electronic configuration = 2 *[1 mark]*

2 E.g. scientists now know that atoms have a positively charged nucleus at the centre (consisting of neutrons and protons) *[1 mark]*, which electrons orbit in shells *[1 mark]*

3 a) E.g. Mendeleev produced a model/table that explained the known data *[1 mark]*. Mendeleev made predictions based on the model *[1 mark]*. Experiments verified his predictions *[1 mark]* allowing his model to be accepted *[1 mark]*.
You'll also get marks if you've discussed peer review in your answer.

b) The electronic configuration of aluminium is 2.8.3 *[1 mark]*. The number of shells is equal to the period number / three occupied electron shells means aluminium is in the third period *[1 mark]*. The number of electrons in the outer shell is equal to the group number / three electrons in the outer shell means aluminium is in the third group *[1 mark]*.

c) Caesium chloride *[1 mark]*
Caesium is more reactive than sodium (because it's closer to the bottom left corner of the periodic table) *[1 mark]* and chlorine is more reactive than iodine (because it's closer to the top right of the periodic table, excluding the noble gases) *[1 mark]*.

Pages 3-6 — Types of Bonding

1 a) Electrons are transferred from magnesium to chlorine *[1 mark]*. The magnesium atoms each lose two electrons to form 2+/Mg²⁺ ions *[1 mark]*. The chlorine atoms each gain one electron to form 1−/Cl⁻ ions *[1 mark]*.
One magnesium/Mg²⁺ ion will combine with two chlorine/Cl⁻ ions to form the neutral, ionic compound MgCl₂

b) Magnesium oxide contains magnesium ions with a 2+ charge and oxide ions with a 2− charge, whereas sodium chloride contains sodium ions with a 1+ charge and chloride ions with a 1− charge *[1 mark]*. So there are stronger ionic bonds / electrostatic forces of attraction in magnesium oxide than in sodium chloride *[1 mark]*, meaning magnesium oxide has a higher melting point *[1 mark]*.

c) Advantage: e.g. it shows the 3D structure / shows ions and bonds *[1 mark]*.
Disadvantage: e.g. it doesn't show distance between ions accurately / doesn't show sizes of ions accurately *[1 mark]*.

d) 2Cs + Cl₂ → 2CsCl *[1 mark for correct formulas, 1 mark for correct balancing]*

2 Solid: the light bulb won't light up *[1 mark]*. This is because, in a solid ionic compound, the ions are held in place so the compound can't conduct electricity *[1 mark]*.
Aqueous: the light bulb will light up *[1 mark]*. This is because, in solution, the ions from the compound separate and are free to move *[1 mark]*.

3 How to grade your answer:
Level 0: There is no relevant information. *[No marks]*
Level 1: There is a brief description of the structures and some of the properties of the substances. *[1 to 2 marks]*
Level 2: There is some comparison of the structures and properties of both substances. There is an attempt to explain how the structures relate to the properties of the materials, but some points are missing or lacking in detail. *[3 to 4 marks]*
Level 3: There is a clear and detailed comparison of the structures and properties of both materials. The properties of both substances have been described in detail, with a clear explanation of how the structures relate to these properties. *[5 to 6 marks]*

Here are some points your answer may include:
Both are giant structures.
Graphite consists of hexagonal layers of carbon atoms, with covalent bonds between atoms within the layers. There are weak forces between the layers.
Metals consist of layers of metal atoms/ions in a regular arrangement surrounded by a sea of delocalised electrons.
Both conduct electricity and both conduct thermal energy.
In graphite, each carbon atom has one delocalised electron which is free to move/transfer thermal energy.
In metals, the outer electrons from each atom are delocalised and free to move through the structure/transfer thermal energy.
Both have high melting and boiling points.
Graphite has many strong covalent bonds that require a lot of energy to break.
Metals have strong metallic bonds that require a lot of energy to break.
Graphite is soft and slippery, because the weak forces between the layers means that the layers can slide over each other.
Metals are malleable (and ductile). This is because the layers of atoms/ions can slide over each other.

4 Fluorine exists as a simple covalent molecule *[1 mark]* in which two fluorine atoms are covalently bonded/share two electrons in order to complete their outer shells *[1 mark]*. During the reaction, the fluorine atoms gain electrons from the Group 1 element atoms *[1 mark]*. This forms fluoride (F⁻) ions that are strongly attracted to the positive Group 1 element ions *[1 mark]*.

5 a) How to grade your answer:
Level 0: There is no relevant information. *[No marks]*
Level 1: Simple statements are made, but the answer is lacking in detail. *[1 to 2 marks]*
Level 2: An explanation is provided demonstrating knowledge of the structures in both substances and some understanding of similarities and differences between them. *[3 to 4 marks]*
Level 3: A detailed and coherent explanation is provided that demonstrates a sound knowledge of the structure and bonding in both substances and a clear understanding of similarities and differences between them. *[5 to 6 marks]*

Here are some points your answer may include:
Diamond contains one type of atom only (carbon).
Silicon dioxide contains silicon and oxygen.
Both are giant structures.
Both have covalent bonds.
In diamond each carbon atom is bonded to four other carbon atoms.
In silicon dioxide each oxygen atom is bonded to two silicon atoms, and each silicon atom is bonded to four oxygen atoms.
In both the arrangement of the bonds is tetrahedral.

b) Yes. Both are giant covalent structures with strong covalent bonds *[1 mark]*. Diamond's hardness comes from its rigid lattice structure, and silicon dioxide has a similar structure *[1 mark]*.

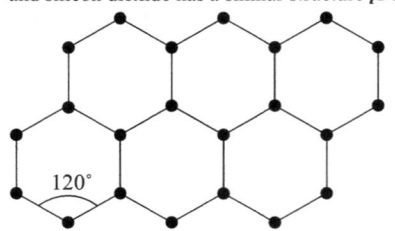

c) *[1 mark for carbon atoms arranged in hexagons, 1 mark for angle of 120°]*

6 Some covalent compounds are simple molecular substances that are made up of a few atoms joined together by covalent bonds *[1 mark]*. These simple molecular substances have weak intermolecular forces, so have very low melting points *[1 mark]*. Other covalent compounds form giant structures with covalent bonds between many atoms *[1 mark]*. These compounds have high melting points as the strong covalent bonds between the atoms require a lot of energy to break *[1 mark]*.

Pages 7-10 — Calculations Involving Masses

1. a) Carbon dioxide is a gas so it escapes into the air/leaves the container (which reduces the mass) *[1 mark]*.
   b) Sodium hydrogencarbonate (NaHCO$_3$) limited the amount of product formed *[1 mark]* because it was completely used up in the reaction (in an excess of citric acid) *[1 mark]*.
   c) Moles of citric acid = mass ÷ M_r = 20.0 ÷ 192 = 0.104... mol
      Molar ratio of citric acid : sodium hydrogencarbonate = 1:3
      so moles of NaHCO$_3$ = 3 × 0.104... = 0.3125 mol
      Mass of NaHCO$_3$ = moles × M_r = 0.3125 × 84 = **26.3 g** (3 s.f.)
      [3 marks for the correct answer to 3 significant figures, otherwise 1 mark for moles of citric acid and 1 mark for moles of sodium hydrogencarbonate]
   d) M_r of sodium citrate = (6 × 12) + (5 × 1) + (7 × 16) + (3 × 23) = 258
      Moles of sodium citrate = mass ÷ M_r = 61.15 ÷ 258 = 0.237... mol
      Molar ratio of sodium citrate : citric acid = 1:1,
      so moles of citric acid = 0.237... mol
      mass of citric acid = moles × M_r = 0.237... × 192 = **45.5 g** (3 s.f.)
      [4 marks for the correct answer to 3 significant figures, otherwise 1 mark for M_r of sodium citrate, 1 mark for moles of sodium citrate and 1 mark for moles of citric acid]

2. a) Moles of MnO$_2$ = mass ÷ M_r = 1.74 ÷ 87 = 0.02 mol
      Mass of XO$_a$ = moles × M_r = 0.02 × 79.5 = **1.59 g**
      [2 marks for the correct answer, otherwise 1 mark for moles of MnO$_2$]
   b) Moles of O$_2$ = mass ÷ M_r = 3.55 ÷ 32 = 0.1109... mol *[1 mark]*
      Moles of XO$_a$ = mass ÷ M_r = 17.65 ÷ 79.5 = 0.2220... mol *[1 mark]*
      0.1109... ÷ 0.1109... = 1, 0.2220... ÷ 0.1109... = 2.00,
      so molar ratio of O$_2$: XO$_a$ = 1:2 *[1 mark]*
      Therefore balanced equation is 2X + O$_2$ → 2XO$_a$
      $a = 1$
      [1 mark for correctly balanced equation and correct value of a]

3. a) E.g. all of the sodium hydrogencarbonate has reacted/been used up/ sodium hydrogencarbonate was the limiting reactant *[1 mark]*.
   b) E.g. take more measurements between 40 cm^3 and 50 cm^3 *[1 mark]*.
   c) Moles of sodium hydrogencarbonate = mass ÷ M_r
      = 12.9 ÷ 84 = 0.153... mol
      Molar ratio of sodium hydrogencarbonate : tartaric acid = 2:1,
      so moles of tartaric acid used in reaction = 0.153... ÷ 2
      = 0.0767... mol
      Mass of tartaric acid used in reaction = moles × M_r
      = 0.0767... × 150 = 11.51... g
      Mass of tartaric acid left = 14.10 – 11.51...
      = 2.582... = **2.6 g** (2 s.f.)
      [4 marks for correct answer to 2 significant figures, otherwise 1 mark for moles of sodium hydrogencarbonate, 1 mark for moles of tartaric acid and 1 mark for mass of tartaric acid]

4. a) C *[1 mark]*
      M_r of sucrose = 342. 6.84 ÷ 342 = 0.02 mol of sucrose, and there are 12 mol of carbon dioxide for every mole of sucrose, so 12 × 0.02 = 0.24 mol of CO$_2$.
   b) Moles of C$_{12}$H$_{22}$O$_{11}$ = mass ÷ M_r = 5.13 ÷ 342 = 0.0150 mol
      Moles of CO = mass ÷ M_r = 3.36 ÷ 28 = 0.120 mol
      Moles of CO$_2$ = mass ÷ M_r = 2.64 ÷ 44 = 0.0600 mol
      Dividing 0.120 and 0.0600 by 0.0150 gives a ratio of 1:8:4
      (C$_{12}$H$_{22}$O$_{11}$: CO : CO$_2$)
      Therefore equation can be balanced as
      C$_{12}$H$_{22}$O$_{11}$ + **8**O$_2$ → **8**CO + **4**CO$_2$ + 11H$_2$O
      [5 marks for correctly balanced equation, otherwise 1 mark for moles of C$_{12}$H$_{22}$O$_{11}$, 1 mark for moles of CO, 1 mark for moles of CO$_2$ and 1 mark for a 1:8:4 molar ratio]
   c) Moles of sucrose = mass ÷ M_r = 12.0 ÷ 342 = 0.0350... mol
      Molar ratio of sucrose : carbon = 1:12, so
      0.0350... × 12 = 0.4210... mol of carbon
      Mass of carbon = moles × A_r = 0.4210... × 12 = 5.0526...
      = **5.05 g** (3 s.f.) *[3 marks for the correct answer to 3 significant figures, otherwise 1 mark for moles of sucrose and 1 mark for moles of carbon]*

Topic 2 — States of Matter and Mixtures

Page 11 — States of Matter

1. a) When a solid is heated its particles gain energy and vibrate more *[1 mark]*. The bonds/forces between the particles are weakened *[1 mark]*. At the melting point, the particles have enough energy to overcome the bonds/forces and break free from their fixed positions *[1 mark]*. They are then arranged randomly and are free to move around each other *[1 mark]*.
   b) Benefit: e.g. the model allows you to compare the arrangement of particles in each state of matter *[1 mark]*.
      Drawback: e.g. the particles are shown as solid inelastic spheres. *[1 mark]*.

2. How to grade your answer:
   Level 0: There is no relevant information. *[No marks]*
   Level 1: Reference is made to the fact that one process is a chemical reaction and the other is a physical state change with incomplete or little explanation of the difference between the two. *[1 to 2 marks]*
   Level 2: The processes are correctly identified as a chemical reaction and a physical state change and some explanation of the difference between the two is given. *[3 to 4 marks]*
   Level 3: The processes are correctly identified and there is a clear understanding of the difference between chemical reactions and physical state changes and why physical state changes are more easily reversible. *[5 to 6 marks]*

   Here are some points your answer may include:
   Decomposition of sodium hydrogencarbonate is a chemical change.
   Sublimation of carbon dioxide is a physical change.
   In a chemical reaction:
   The bonds between atoms break.
   New bonds form between the atoms of reactants to produce different substances (products).
   There is usually no straightforward way to turn products back into reactants — the process may require several steps.
   In a physical state change:
   The bonds/forces between molecules are broken (or weakened).
   The substances remain the same.
   To return the substance back into its original state requires a change in temperature (and/or pressure).
   A physical state change is more easily reversible than a chemical reaction.
   So the sublimation of carbon dioxide will be easier to reverse than the decomposition of sodium hydrogencarbonate.

Pages 12-14 — Separating Mixtures

1. a) Technique 1: Filtration *[1 mark]*
      Explanation: Filtering separates the silicon dioxide from the copper sulfate solution *[1 mark]*.
      Technique 2: Crystallisation *[1 mark]*
      Explanation: Crystals of copper sulfate will form as water evaporates *[1 mark]*.
   b) The boiling points are too close together for simple distillation to be used *[1 mark]*. Fractional distillation allows substances with close boiling points to be separated *[1 mark]* because it provides a temperature gradient/is hot at the bottom and cool at the top *[1 mark]*, so only substances with a specific boiling point can reach the top (and be separated off) without condensing and running back into the flask *[1 mark]*.
   c) Chromatography *[1 mark]*. Unlike distillation, this doesn't involve heating the mixture *[1 mark]*.

2. a) E.g. 120 mg = 0.120 g
      Percentage = (0.120 ÷ 5) × 100 = **2.4%**
      [2 marks for correct answer, otherwise 1 mark for either converting 120 mg to g or 5.0 g to mg.]
   b) The different substances will be distributed differently between the mobile phase/solvent and the stationary phase/paper *[1 mark]*. The substances will separate because they spend different amounts of time in the mobile phase/they have different solubilities in the mobile phase *[1 mark]* and therefore move different distances up the paper *[1 mark]*.
   c) Distance moved by propyl paraben = 1.8 cm
      Distance moved by solvent = 4.2 cm
      R_f = 1.8 ÷ 4.2 = **0.43** (2 s.f.) (allow between 0.40 and 0.46)
      [3 marks for correct answer, otherwise 1 mark for both distances correctly measured within 0.1 cm and 1 mark for correct equation.]

Answers

d) Distance moved = 0.52 × 4.2 = **2.2 cm** (2 s.f.)
Spot drawn at 2.2 cm from baseline.
[3 marks for correct answer, correctly marked on diagram, otherwise 1 mark for correct equation to calculate distance and 1 mark for 2.2 cm]

e) The contaminant is not pure *[1 mark]*. It melts over a range of temperatures and pure substances melt at specific temperatures *[1 mark]*.

3 a) In everday use 'pure' can mean clean/natural, whereas in science 'pure' specifically means that something is entirely made up from a single element or compound *[1 mark]*.

b) Run **Z** alongside pure samples of **A**, **B**, and **C** *[1 mark]*. If the spot from **A**, **B** or **C** moves the same distance as a spot from **Z**, then it indicates that this may be the contaminant / if the R_f value for **A**, **B** or **C** matches that of a component of **Z**, then it indicates that this may be the contaminant *[1 mark]*.

c) Repeat the experiment using different solvents *[1 mark]*. Calculate new R_f values for the substances in each solvent, and see if they still match *[1 mark]*.

Just because the R_f values of two substances match in one solvent doesn't mean they're the same substance. You need to calculate their R_f values in multiple solvents — if they don't match in all of them, they aren't the same.

Page 15 — Water Treatment

1 a) Any two from: filtration / sedimentation / chlorination *[1 mark for each]*.

b) Tap water contains ions *[1 mark]*. Ions can interfere with chemical reactions, potentially giving false results *[1 mark]*. Deionised water should be used instead *[1 mark]*.

c) How to grade your answer:
Level 0: There is no relevant information. *[No marks]*
Level 1: There is a brief description of the pros and cons of the methods. However, the answer lacks detail and no attempt at a conclusion is made. *[1 to 2 marks]*
Level 2: There is some description of the pros and cons of the methods and an attempt is made at drawing a conclusion. *[3 to 4 marks]*
Level 2: There is a clear, logical evaluation of the methods with a reasoned conclusion. *[5 to 6 marks]*

Here are some points your answer may include:
Waste water from other processes will need to be treated by the company before releasing it into the environment anyway, so it is more cost effective to use it twice before treating it.
The company would need to produce enough waste water from other processes to use in processing the ore.
Waste water may need treating before it is suitable to be reused.
The company would need to provide a way of piping the water between locations.
The distillation of seawater requires a large amount of energy.
The distillation of seawater is an expensive process.
Distilling seawater would require a nearby source of seawater, otherwise it would have to be transported in.
If the mine is located in a region with insufficient ground water sources, distillation may be the only option to produce enough water.
The distillation of seawater is not a suitable method for producing large volumes of water.
If purified/potable water is not required for the mine's processes, distillation of seawater might be an unnecessary step.
The use of waste water from other processes would involve the least cost and least energy input.

Topic 3 — Chemical Changes

Pages 16-17 — Acids

1 a) Boric acid *[1 mark]*
b) The concentration of hydrogen ions in the sulfuric acid solution is 100 times greater than in the oxalic acid solution *[1 mark]*.

For every decrease of 1 on the pH scale, the concentration of H⁺ ions increases by a factor of 10. There is a difference of 2 between the pH of the oxalic acid and the pH of the sulfuric acid, so the concentration of H⁺ ions has increased by a factor of 10^2 = 100.

c) The pH will decrease *[1 mark]* because the remaining solution is more concentrated *[1 mark]*.

The solution is more concentrated because there is the same amount of acid in a smaller volume of water.

2 a) A *[1 mark]*
The volumes and the concentrations of the solutions are the same, so they both have the same number of acid molecules and the same number of water molecules. Carbonic acid is a weak acid, though, so it only partially dissociates to release H⁺ ions. This means it has a lower concentration of H⁺ ions, so the pH is higher.

b) The concentration of hydrogen ions will be lower than the concentration of acid molecules *[1 mark]* because carbonic acid is a weak acid and so only a small number of the acid molecules will dissociate to produce hydrogen ions *[1 mark]*.

3 a) i) sodium *[1 mark]*
ii) Place a lighted splint into the gas *[1 mark]*. If the gas is hydrogen then it will burn with a squeaky pop *[1 mark]*.

b) i) $Mg(OH)_2 + 2HNO_3 \rightarrow Mg(NO_3)_2 + 2H_2O$
[1 mark for correct equation, 1 mark for balancing]
ii) There will be bubbles/fizzing in the second flask (but not in the first flask) *[1 mark]*, because carbon dioxide gas is produced *[1 mark]*.
iii) magnesium oxide/MgO *[1 mark]*

c) E.g. **MX** is an alkali *[1 mark]*, because it reacts with the acid to neutralise it (as shown by the rise in pH) *[1 mark]* and it is soluble in water *[1 mark]*. **MX** can't be a metal carbonate, because a gas is not produced when **MX** reacts with acid (as shown by the lack of bubbles) *[1 mark]*.

Pages 18-19 — Electrolysis

1 B *[1 mark]*
Molten magnesium chloride only contains magnesium ions and chloride ions. The positively charged magnesium ions are attracted to the cathode, where they are reduced to magnesium. The negatively charged chloride ions are attracted to the anode, where they are oxidised to chlorine.

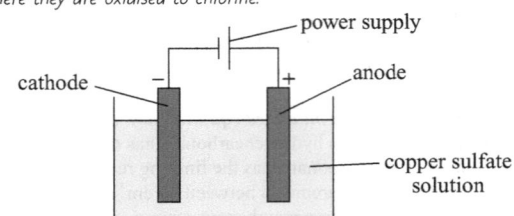

2 a) [Diagram showing electrolysis cell with power supply, cathode (−), anode (+), and copper sulfate solution]
[1 mark for correct diagram, 1 mark for correct labels]

b) Copper is produced at the cathode *[1 mark]* because copper is less reactive than hydrogen *[1 mark]*. Oxygen and water are produced at the anode *[1 mark]* because the solution does not contain halide ions *[1 mark]*.

c) Anode: $4OH^- \rightarrow O_2 + 2H_2O + 4e^-$ *[1 mark]*
Cathode: $Cu^{2+} + 2e^- \rightarrow Cu$ *[1 mark]*

d) Cu^{2+} *[1 mark]*, because it gains electrons *[1 mark]*.

3 a) A *[1 mark]*
All four options produce a gas at the anode. Dilute sulfuric acid, aqueous potassium sulfate and aqueous sodium chloride all produce hydrogen gas at the cathode. Molten zinc chloride produces zinc at the cathode, because, since it isn't in aqueous solution, there are no competing hydrogen ions.

b) The anode/positive electrode, because the ion is being oxidised *[1 mark]*, and during electrolysis oxidation always happens at the anode/positive electrode *[1 mark]*.

4 How to grade your answer:
Level 0: There is no relevant information. *[No marks]*
Level 1: Simple statements about electrolysis are made. The answer lacks detail and the points are not linked. *[1 to 2 marks]*
Level 2: The answer provides a description of how electrolysis can be used to extract sodium from solid sodium hydroxide. However some explanation may be undeveloped and some points are not linked. The answer includes an attempt at writing both half equations, but they may not be entirely correct. *[3 to 4 marks]*
Level 3: There is a clear and detailed explanation of how electrolysis can be used to extract sodium from solid sodium hydroxide, including correct half equations. The answer follows a logical structure and points are linked together. *[5 to 6 marks]*

Here are some points your answer may include:
Solid sodium hydroxide cannot be electrolysed because the ions are not free to move.
The sodium hydroxide must be molten before it can be electrolysed, so the ions can move and conduct electricity.
You cannot dissolve the sodium hydroxide in water, because water contains hydrogen/H⁺ ions.

Answers

Sodium is more reactive than hydrogen, so if hydrogen/H$^+$ ions were present they would be reduced instead of the sodium/Na$^+$ ions.
The electrodes must be inert, so they don't degrade/react with the electrolyte.
The positively charged sodium ions move towards the cathode/negative electrode.
At the cathode/negative electrode, the sodium ions are reduced/gain electrons to form sodium metal.
Na$^+$ + e$^-$ → Na.
The negatively charged hydroxide ions move towards the anode/positive electrode.
At the anode/positive electrode, the hydroxide ions are oxidised/lose electrons to form oxygen (and water).
4OH$^-$ → O$_2$ + 2H$_2$O + 4e$^-$.

Topic 4 — Extracting Metals and Equilibria

Pages 20-25 — Metals and Sustainability

1 a) E.g. titanium does not react with sodium chloride/sodium compounds *[1 mark]*.
   b) E.g. iron does not need to be removed from rutile / there is a higher proportion of titanium in rutile *[1 mark]*.
   c) Any two from: e.g. titanium chloride needs to be purified / there are many stages / electrolysis requires a lot of energy *[2 marks]*.
   d) i) TiCl$_4$ + 2Mg → 2MgCl$_2$ + Ti *[1 mark for correct formulae of reactants and products, 1 mark for balancing]*
      ii) Oxidised: magnesium/Mg *[1 mark]*
          Reduced: titanium/ Ti^{2+} *[1 mark]*
2 a) i) No reaction would take place *[1 mark]* because copper is below hydrogen in the reactivity series (therefore cannot displace it) *[1 mark]*.
      ii) Zn + 2H$^+$ → Zn^{2+} + H$_2$ *[1 mark]*
The chloride ions aren't included because they're the same on both sides of the equation.
      iii) H$^+$ *[1 mark]*
   b) Equation: Mg$_{(s)}$ + CuSO$_{4(aq)}$ → MgSO$_{4(aq)}$ + Cu$_{(s)}$ *[1 mark for correct formulae of products, 1 mark for state symbols]*
      Explanation: The orange-brown solid is a coating of copper, which is displaced from the solution *[1 mark]*. The colour fades as blue copper sulfate solution reacts to form colourless magnesium sulfate solution *[1 mark]*.
   c) There is only a small difference in reactivity/calcium is only a little bit more reactive than magnesium *[1 mark]*.
   d) A *[1 mark]*
Metal Z reacts vigorously with acids and water, which is a typical property of metals that are near the top of the reactivity series.
3 a) How to grade your answer:
   Level 0: There is no relevant information. *[No marks]*
   Level 1: Simple statements about the environmental impact of either reduction of copper ores or bioleaching are made. The answer lacks detail/understanding and no clear conclusion is made. *[1 to 2 marks]*
   Level 2: The answer shows reasonable understanding of the environmental impact of both methods. However some points may be undeveloped or incorrect. An attempt at a conclusion is made. *[3 to 4 marks]*
   Level 3: A detailed and coherent answer is given that uses all of the information to fully evaluate the environmental impact of both methods The answer has a logical structure and is used to support a reasoned conclusion. *[5 to 6 marks]*
Here are some points your answer may include:
Reduction of copper ores:
Can only use high-grade copper ores, which are rarer than low-grade ores. Copper will have to be mined to supply this, which comes with its own environmental impacts, e.g. destruction of landscapes, increased burning of fossil fuels for energy/transportation.
The production of the reducing agent/carbon may also involve mining, which will damage landscapes and use up fossil fuels.
Large volumes of water will require energy in order to be piped to the refinery.
The water will also need to be treated before it can be returned to the environment.
Energy will be required for crushing and grinding of the ore, as well as the transportation of the ore through each step of the process.
Large amounts of energy will be required for the high-temperature heating of the ore.
The energy for these processes may be provided by fossil fuels.
Fossil fuels are a finite resource that release pollutants such as carbon dioxide (a greenhouse gas) when burned.
Large amounts of waste are produced, which is not recycled.
Low grade/waste ore may end up at landfill sites.
Several waste products are gases, which may be hard to capture before they are released to the environment.
Carbon dioxide is produced directly by the process. Carbon dioxide is a greenhouse gas that can lead to global warming.
Carbon monoxide and sulfur dioxide are produced, which are harmful pollutants.
Bioleaching:
Acidic waste could contaminate water supplies/lakes, which could endanger aquatic species.
The aqueous waste will have to be treated before it can be released, which will require energy.
The products still have to be extracted from aqueous solution, which will require energy/other raw materials.
Low-grade ores can be used, which reduces the need to mine more copper.
The materials for the process do not require large amounts of energy to produce.
Low temperatures can be used, so less energy is required.
Overall, less energy is required and less waste is produced by bioleaching than by reduction of copper ores, so bioleaching has the smaller impact on the environment.
   b) E.g. lots of copper can be produced at once, because the process is fast / less ore is needed to produce the same mass of copper than with bioleaching *[1 mark]*.
4 a)

Reactivity Series
Barium
Calcium
Aluminium
Iron
Nickel
Lead

[3 marks for all four correct, otherwise 2 marks for two or 1 mark for one]
   b) Carbon would be placed between aluminium and iron *[1 mark]* because carbon can only reduce metals that are less reactive than itself *[1 mark]* and aluminium is extracted by electrolysis *[1 mark]*.
5 a) Electrolysis *[1 mark]*.
   b) E.g. by recycling chlorine (a by-product) to form hydrochloric acid *[1 mark]*.
6 E.g. Bioleaching is more cost-effective than mining, whereas phytoextraction is more expensive, so it'll be easier for the company to make profits using bioleaching *[1 mark]*. The pollutants released by phytoextraction include greenhouse gases, which are difficult to capture. The substances released by bioleaching are toxic, but might be easier to capture / remove from the environment than greenhouse gases *[1 mark]*. Both processes are slow, so the rate of extraction will not affect the company's choice *[1 mark]*. Bioleaching is the better choice for the company as it is more cost-effective than phytoextraction and its environmental impact is likely to be easier to manage *[1 mark]*.
You might have made different points here — that's okay, the key thing is to use the information given in the question. Back up each of your points, and don't give a conclusion without supporting it with evidence from the data.
7 a) How to grade your answer:
   Level 0: There is no relevant information. *[No marks]*
   Level 1: Simple statements about the environmental impact of either bioplastic bottles or traditional plastic bottles are made. The answer lacks detail/understanding and no clear conclusion is made. *[1 to 2 marks]*
   Level 2: The answer shows reasonable understanding of the environmental impact of both types of bottle. However some points may be undeveloped or incorrect. An attempt at a conclusion is made. *[3 to 4 marks]*
   Level 3: A detailed and coherent answer is given that uses all of the information to fully evaluate the environmental impact of both types of bottle. The answer has a logical structure and is used to support a reasoned conclusion. *[5 to 6 marks]*

Here are some points your answer may include:
Using waste cooking oil is better for the environment than extracting and processing crude oil, as the cooking oil would be disposed of otherwise and processing crude oil requires lots of energy.
Waste cooking oil comes from a renewable resource, whereas crude oil is a non-renewable resource.
The bioplastic can biodegrade under the right conditions, whereas traditional plastic bottles do not biodegrade at all, and would therefore be disposed of in landfill, which would pollute the land.
There is no quantitative data included in the life cycle assessments, so it is not possible to give an objective comparison of, e.g. the amount of energy required in the manufacturing processes.
The life cycle assessments may be biased towards the use of bioplastic instead of traditional plastic, as there is no information about who they were written by.
The life cycle assessments don't include additional factors such as the cost of manufacturing or any waste products that are produced during the manufacturing process that might damage the environment.
The life cycle assessments do not specify how many times each type of bottle may be reused. It might be that the bioplastic bottle can only be reused once but the traditional plastic bottle can be reused multiple times, which would be better for the environment as fewer bottles would need to be disposed of in the same amount of time.
The life cycle assessments do not mention that the traditional plastic bottle could potentially be recycled.
There is no information on how long the bioplastic bottle takes to biodegrade, or if it produces toxic products when it does so, which could be damaging to the environment.
The life cycle assessments do not include any information on what happens to the bioplastic bottle if it does not biodegrade under the correct conditions, and the potential effect on the environment.
The life cycle assessments give some information that supports the student's conclusion, but more information would be required to confirm whether their conclusion is correct.

b) E.g. growing new crops instead of using existing waste cooking oil means that the waste cooking oil will be disposed of instead of being reused *[1 mark]*. Growing new crops specifically to make bioplastic would require more energy and resources than using waste oil / may result in deforestation and habitat loss / would require land that might otherwise be used for growing food, which will affect food prices and availability for the local population *[1 mark]*.

Pages 26-27 — Reversible Reactions and Equilibria

1 a) As the reaction progresses, the concentration of iodine and hydrogen gas decreases, so the forward reaction slows down *[1 mark]*, but as more hydrogen iodide is made, the backwards reaction speeds up *[1 mark]*. After a while, the forward and backward reactions will be going at the same rate (so the reaction will have reached equilibrium) *[1 mark]*.
Remember that in a closed system nothing can leave or enter — this is what allows the system to reach equilibrium.

b) The equilibrium position would move to the right *[1 mark]* in order to use up the extra reactant *[1 mark]*.
c) Time = 80 seconds *[1 mark]*
This is the time when both lines become horizontal and therefore the concentrations of products and reactants do not change.
d) A *[1 mark]*
The equilibrium would move to the left to increase the concentration of hydrogen gas. More iodine (the purple vapour) would be formed.
e) The backward reaction is exothermic *[1 mark]*, because more iodine has formed/the equilibrium has shifted to the left *[1 mark]*, and lowering the temperature of a reaction at equilibrium favours the exothermic direction *[1 mark]*.

2 The percentage yield of SO_3 increases as the temperature decreases/the forward reaction is exothermic *[1 mark]* therefore low temperatures will cause the equilibrium to move to the right and provide the maximum percentage yield (in terms of temperature) *[1 mark]*. There are more molecules of gas on the reactant side than on the product side *[1 mark]* therefore a high pressure will cause the equilibrium to move to the right and provide the highest percentage yield (in terms of pressure) *[1 mark]*.

Topic 5 — Separate Chemistry 1

Page 28 — Transition Metals, Alloys and Corrosion

1 a) Copper is the most suitable metal for water storage tanks *[1 mark]* as it is the least reactive and will not corrode in contact with water *[1 mark]*.
b) How to grade your answer:
Level 0: No relevant information. *[No marks]*
Level 1: Simple statements are given about methods used to prevent corrosion. No reference is made to the use of magnesium in particular. *[1 to 2 marks]*
Level 2: The answer gives a comparison of the use of magnesium blocks and other methods used to prevent corrosion. Some reference is made to the use of magnesium in particular. *[3 to 4 marks]*
Level 3: The answer gives a detailed and coherent comparison of the use of magnesium blocks and other methods used to prevent corrosion, which discusses the advantages and disadvantages of the methods named. The position of magnesium in the reactivity series is used to justify its use in the blocks. *[5 to 6 marks]*

Here are some points your answer may include:
The magnesium blocks are used for sacrificial protection to prevent the steel from rusting.
Magnesium is more reactive than iron so reacts in preference to the steel.
Metals above magnesium would be too reactive / react with the water.
Metals below iron (copper) would not be reactive enough, so the iron would rust.
Paint, oil or grease could be used to create a barrier between the steel and air/oxygen/water.
Paint can be used on large structures and can be decorative, but may need to be reapplied on a regular basis.
Oil and grease is usually used to protect moving parts and will need to be reapplied frequently to the ship.
Reapplication of paint, oil or grease would require the ship to be taken out of the water / put in a dry dock.
Galvanising means coating an iron object in zinc. Zinc is more reactive than iron, so galvanising forms a protective barrier, but is also a method of sacrificial protection.
It would be practically impossible to galvanise the whole ship and galvanising individual parts would be time-consuming and costly.

c) E.g. when iron corrodes, a soft crumbly solid (rust) forms *[1 mark]*. This flakes off, leaving more iron available to react with air and therefore all the iron will eventually rust *[1 mark]*, whereas the aluminium won't be completely destroyed by corrosion *[1 mark]*.

Pages 29-30 — Titrations

1 a) C *[1 mark]*
When calculating the mean volume added in a titration, you should only use concordant results. All the other values are anomalous results and shouldn't be used in your calculation. Concordant results are within 0.1 cm³ of each other.

b) Moles of sulfuric acid = concentration × volume
= 0.500 × (25 ÷ 1000) = 0.0125 mol
Molar ratio of sodium hydroxide to sulfuric acid is 2:1,
so moles of sodium hydroxide = 0.0125 × 2 = 0.0250
Concentration of sodium hydroxide = moles ÷ volume
= 0.0250 ÷ (23.40 ÷ 1000) = 1.06837... = **1.07 mol dm⁻³**
[3 marks for correct answer given to 3 significant figures, otherwise 1 mark for moles of sulfuric acid, 1 mark for moles of sodium hydroxide]

2 a) 13.0 cm³ *[1 mark]*
This is the volume of HCl added when the pH = 7.
b) Reaction equation: NaOH + HCl → NaCl + H_2O
Moles of hydrochloric acid = concentration × volume
= (35 ÷ 1000) × 0.25 = 0.00875 mol
Molar ratio of sodium hydroxide : hydrochloric acid = 1:1,
so moles of sodium hydroxide = moles of hydrochloric acid
= 0.00875 mol
Mass of sodium hydroxide = moles × M_r = 0.00875 × 40
= **0.35 g** *[4 marks for the correct answer, otherwise 1 mark for 0.00875 moles of hydrochloric acid, 1 mark for a 1:1 molar ratio and 1 mark for 0.00875 moles of sodium hydroxide]*

79

Pages 31-32 — Atom Economy and Percentage Yield

1. a) M_r of $CuCO_3$ = 63.5 + 12 + (3 × 16) = 123.5
   Moles of $CuCO_3$ = mass ÷ M_r = 12.0 ÷ 123.5 = 0.09716... mol
   Molar ratio of $CuCO_3$: CuO = 1:1, so
   moles of CuO = moles of $CuCO_3$ = 0.09716... mol
   Theoretical yield of CuO = moles × M_r = 0.09716... × 79.5
   = 7.724... g
   Percentage yield = (actual yield of product ÷ theoretical yield of product) × 100
   = (5.10 ÷ 7.724...) × 100 = 66.022... = **66.0%** (3 s.f.)
   [6 marks for the correct answer, otherwise 1 mark for M_r of $CuCO_3$, 1 mark for moles of $CuCO_3$, 1 mark for moles of CuO, 1 mark for theoretical yield of CuO and 1 mark for equation for percentage yield]

   b) Atom economy = (relative formula mass of desired products ÷ relative formula mass of all reactants) × 100
   Relative formula mass of all reactants = 79.5 + 98 = 177.5
   Relative formula mass of desired product/$CuSO_4$ = 159.5
   Atom economy = (159.5 ÷ 177.5) × 100 = 89.8591...
   = **89.86%** *[3 marks for the correct answer given to 2 decimal places, otherwise 1 mark for correct relative formula mass of all reactants and 1 mark for correct equation for atom economy]*
   $CuSO_4$ is the only desired product from the reaction. You could have also divided by the relative formula mass of all the products, which is the same as the relative formula mass of all the reactants.

   c) Some product will be lost at each stage of the process *[1 mark]*.
   So reducing the number of steps is likely to increase the yield by reducing the amount of product lost *[1 mark]*.

2. a) Atom economy = (relative formula mass of desired products ÷ relative formula mass of all reactants) × 100
   Relative formula mass of all reactants
   = 80 + (2 × 71) + 12 + (2 × 24) = 282
   Relative atomic mass of desired product = 48
   Atom economy = (48 ÷ 282) × 100 = 17.021... = **17.0%**
   [3 marks for the correct answer, otherwise 1 mark for correct relative formula mass of all reactants and 1 mark for correct equation for atom economy]
   You could also divide by the relative formula mass of all the products, which is the same as the relative formula mass of all the reactants.

   b) How to grade your answer:
   Level 0: No relevant information. *[No marks]*
   Level 1: Simple statements are given relating to the problems with either or both of the methods. No connection is made between the problems and the impact on the level of titanium production. *[1 to 2 marks]*
   Level 2: The drawbacks of the methods are described well, though there is little or incomplete explanation as to why they result in titanium only being used for limited purposes. *[3 to 4 marks]*
   Level 3: A detailed and coherent explanation is given that acknowledges the disadvantages of both methods from an industrial point of view, and shows an understanding of how this leads to titanium only being used for specialised purposes. *[5 to 6 marks]*
   Here are some points your answer may include:
   The atom economies of both methods are low.
   Higher atom economy is desirable because of sustainability / economic reasons / there would be less wasted products.
   Method 1 produces more waste products ($MgCl_2$ and CO_2) compared to Method 2 (O_2).
   Low atom economies mean the processes aren't very 'green' / could have negative environmental impacts.
   Method 1 must be carried out under an argon atmosphere, which could be expensive.
   Method 1 requires chlorine and magnesium, which must be extracted themselves.
   A lot of energy would be required to melt the salt so it can be used as the electrolyte in Method 2.
   Both methods require high temperatures, and therefore a lot of energy.
   Both methods are (highly) expensive.
   Both methods are slow, and therefore not ideal for industry.
   The high cost and low efficiency of the methods mean that it requires a lot of money to extract titanium metal.
   This limits the uses of titanium to uses for which there is no cheaper/more readily available alternative.

Pages 33-34 — Chemical Reactions in Industry

1. a) Ammonia has a higher boiling point than the other two gases *[1 mark]*.

   b) How to grade your answer:
   Level 0: There is no relevant information. *[No marks]*
   Level 1: Simple statements about the choice of temperature and/or pressure are made. The answer lacks detail and understanding. *[1 to 2 marks]*
   Level 2: An explanation is given showing a reasonable understanding of the principles involved in selecting a temperature and pressure with consideration of both yield and rate. However, explanations may be incomplete or imprecise. *[3 to 4 marks]*
   Level 3: A detailed and coherent explanation is given, showing a sound understanding of the principles involved in selecting a temperature and pressure with full consideration of both yield and rate. Explanation involves linked ideas and logical reasoning. *[5 to 6 marks]*
   Here are some points your answer may include:
   The commercially used conditions are 450 °C and 200 atm.
   From the graph, a low temperature gives the highest yield of ammonia.
   Low temperatures give the highest yields of ammonia because the forward reaction is exothermic.
   A low temperature gives a low rate of reaction.
   A high temperature increases the cost of energy required.
   From the graph, a high pressure gives the highest yield of ammonia.
   There are more moles/molecules on the left hand (reactants) side.
   An increase in pressure causes the equilibrium to shift towards the side with the smaller number of molecules.
   A higher pressure gives a higher rate of reaction.
   A higher pressure requires more energy to create it.
   Compromise is used for both temperature and pressure to balance the yield with cost of energy and rate.
   An iron catalyst is used to make the reaction go faster. This allows the equilibrium to be reached sooner but does not affect its position.

2. a) $NH_3 + HNO_3 \rightarrow NH_4NO_3$ *[1 mark]*

   b) (38 ÷ 100) × 500 = 190 g (of the fertiliser is N, P and K)
   14 + 11 + 27 = 52
   Mass of N = (14 ÷ 52) × 190 = **51.2 g**
   Mass of P = (11 ÷ 52) × 190 = **40.2 g**
   Mass of K = (27 ÷ 52) × 190 = **98.7 g**
   [3 marks for the correct answers, otherwise 1 mark for the correct total mass of N, P and K, 1 mark for 52]

   c) Method 1 is more suitable for use in industry than Method 2 because it can be done on a larger scale *[1 mark]* and it uses more concentrated reactants, so will have a faster rate of reaction/production *[1 mark]*. Although Method 2 produces a pure product, crystallisation is slow and therefore not suitable for industry/large scale production *[1 mark]*.

Page 35 — Calculations with Gases

1. a) Moles of oxygen gas = volume ÷ 24 = (60 ÷ 1000) ÷ 24
   = **0.0025 mol** *[2 marks for the correct answer, otherwise 1 mark for correct equation to calculate moles of oxygen gas]*

   b) E.g. moles of hydrogen peroxide in 1 dm^3 = mass ÷ M_r
   = 60 ÷ 34 = 1.7647... mol
   Moles in 100 cm^3 (0.1 dm^3) = 1.7647... ÷ 10 = 0.17647... mol
   Molar ratio of hydrogen peroxide : oxygen gas = 2:1, so
   moles of oxygen gas = 0.17647... ÷ 2 = 0.088235... mol
   Volume of oxygen gas = moles × 24 = 0.088235... × 24
   = **2.1 dm^3** (2 s.f.)
   [4 marks for the correct answer, otherwise 1 mark for moles of hydrogen peroxide in 1 dm^3, 1 mark for moles of hydrogen peroxide in 100 cm^3, and 1 mark for moles of oxygen gas]
   Alternative valid working gets the marks too — for example, you could work out the mass of H_2O_2 in 100 cm^3 in order find the moles of H_2O_2 in 100 cm^3.

2. Mass of gas = 200 − 186 = 14 g
   Moles of gas = mass ÷ M_r = 14 ÷ 44 = 0.318... mol
   Volume of gas = moles × molar volume = 0.318... × 24
   = 7.636... dm^3 = **7.6 dm^3** *[3 marks for the correct answer to 2 significant figures, otherwise 1 mark for the correct number of moles and 1 mark for correct equation for volume]*

Answers

80

Page 36 — Chemical Cells and Fuel Cells

1 How to grade your answer:
   Level 0: There is no relevant information. *[No marks]*
   Level 1: There is a basic comparison of the two technologies, but not all the information has been referred to. A recommendation has been given, but with little explanation of why this technology should be used. *[1 to 2 marks]*
   Level 2: There is a good comparison of the two technologies, but some points are missing or lacking in detail. A recommendation has been given, with some explanation of why this technology should be used. *[3 to 4 marks]*
   Level 3: A clear recommendation is given. The recommendation is supported by a thorough analysis of the advantages and disadvantages of both technologies. *[5 to 6 marks]*

   Here are some points your answer may include:
   Both contain hazardous flammable materials.
   Hydrogen fuel cells use a gas, which can be harder to store than solids.
   Gases have large volumes, so hydrogen would need to be compressed/absorbed.
   Lithium reacts (exothermically) with water, so if the battery was damaged, an uncontrolled reaction could occur if exposed to water.
   Transferring hydrogen requires specialist skills, so it could be more expensive to use.
   Recharging lithium batteries uses common technology and is well understood.
   Hydrogen fuel cells have a lower cost per kilowatt hour.
   Lithium batteries last twice as long as fuel cells.
   A lithium rechargeable battery would therefore be more suitable for use in a mobile phone.

2 a) The reaction within the fuel cell which produces the voltage across the cell will stop when one of the reactants/hydrogen is used up *[1 mark]*
   b) E.g. hydrogen is a gas so requires more space to store it than liquid or solid fuels (e.g. coal, petrol) *[1 mark]*. Hydrogen is very explosive so is difficult to store safely *[1 mark]*. Hydrogen is often produced using fossil fuels (either as a reactant or to produce electricity for the electrolysis of water) *[1 mark]*.

Any other valid reasons would also get marks.

Mixed Questions for Paper 1

Pages 37-41 — Mixed Questions for Paper 1

1 a) i) Relative formula mass = $(3 × 40) + (2(31 + (4 × 16)))$ = **310** *[2 marks for the correct answer, otherwise 1 mark for correct working]*
      ii) $6CaO + P_4O_{10} \rightarrow 2Ca_3(PO_4)_2$ *[1 mark]*
      iii) Measure the melting point *[1 mark]*. If the sample melts over a range of temperatures then it is contaminated/impure *[1 mark]*.
   b) Reduce the pressure *[1 mark]*. There are more moles of gas on the right-hand side of the equation, so reducing the pressure will cause the equilibrium to shift to the right, forming more calcium oxide (and carbon dioxide) *[1 mark]*.

2 a) i) Moles of sulfuric acid = concentration × volume
         = $2.00 × (22.5 ÷ 1000)$ = 0.0450 mol
         Molar ratio of potassium carbonate : sulfuric acid = 1:1, so moles of potassium carbonate = moles of sulfuric acid
         = 0.0450 mol
         Concentration of potassium carbonate solution
         = moles ÷ volume = $0.0450 ÷ (25.0 ÷ 1000)$ = **1.80 mol dm^{-3}**
         [4 marks for the correct answer to 3 s.f., otherwise 1 mark for moles of sulfuric acid, 1 mark for moles of potassium carbonate and 1 mark for equation to calculate concentration of potassium carbonate]
         If the concentration is given in mol dm^{-3} then make sure you convert any volumes to dm^3.
      ii) moles of potassium carbonate = concentration × volume
         = $2.00 × (25 ÷ 1000)$ = 0.05 mol
         M_r of potassium carbonate (K_2CO_3)
         = $(2 × 39) + (1 × 12) + (3 × 16)$ = 138
         Mass = moles × M_r = $0.05 × 138$ = **6.9 g**
         [3 marks for the correct answer, otherwise 1 mark for moles of potassium carbonate and 1 mark for M_r of potassium carbonate]

   b) Moles of potassium carbonate = mass ÷ M_r = $0.552 ÷ 138$
      = 0.00400 mol
      Molar ratio of potassium carbonate : carbon dioxide = 1:1 so moles of carbon dioxide = moles of potassium carbonate
      = 0.00400 mol
      Volume of carbon dioxide = moles × 24.0 = $0.00400 × 24.0$
      = **0.0960 dm^3**
      [3 marks for the correct answer, otherwise 1 mark for moles of potassium carbonate and 1 mark for moles of carbon dioxide]
   c) i) Moles of potassium carbonate = mass ÷ M_r
         = $5.87 ÷ 138$ = 0.04253... mol
         Molar ratio of potassium carbonate : sulfuric acid = 1:1, so moles of sulfuric acid = 0.04253... mol
         Volume of sulfuric acid = moles ÷ concentration
         = $0.04253... ÷ 2.00$ = 0.02126... dm^3 = **21.3 cm^3** (3 s.f.)
         [4 marks for correct answer to 3 s.f., otherwise 1 mark for moles of potassium carbonate, 1 mark for moles of sulfuric acid and 1 mark for volume of sulfuric acid in dm^3]
      ii) C *[1 mark]*

3 a) Oxygen gas/O_2 *[1 mark]*
      Hydroxide/OH^- ions from the water molecules of the aqueous solution are oxidised/gain electrons to form O_2 *[1 mark]*.
   b) $4OH^- \rightarrow 2H_2O + O_2 + 4e^-$
      [1 mark for correctly identifying water as the other product, 1 mark for the correct balanced equation]
   c) $Cu^{2+} + 2e^- \rightarrow Cu$ *[1 mark]*
   d) Copper is still produced at the negative electrode/cathode *[1 mark]* because copper is less reactive than both hydrogen and potassium *[1 mark]*. Chlorine is produced at the positive electrode/anode *[1 mark]* because a halogen is always produced if a halide ion is present in the solution *[1 mark]*.

4 a) i) $Mn + H_2SO_4 \rightarrow MnSO_4 + H_2$
         [1 mark for each correctly identified product]
      ii) The solid manganese will disappear as it reacts/dissolves *[1 mark]*. There will be bubbles of gas, because hydrogen gas is produced *[1 mark]*. The solution will change colour, because $MnSO_4$ is produced and solutions of transition metal compounds are typically coloured *[1 mark]*.
   b) No reaction would occur *[1 mark]*, because copper is even less reactive than iron (and iron is not reactive enough to displace the manganese from manganese sulfate) *[1 mark]*.
   An element can only be displaced from its salt by a more reactive element.

5 a) Moles of hydrochloric acid = concentration × volume
      = $1 × (50 ÷ 1000)$ = 0.05 mol
      Molar ratio of hydrochloric acid : hydrogen = 2:1, so
      Moles of H_2 = $0.05 ÷ 2$ = 0.025 mol
      Volume = $24 × 0.025$ = **0.60 dm^3**
      [3 marks for the correct answer, otherwise 1 mark for correct moles of hydrochloric acid and 1 mark for correct moles of hydrogen]
   b) Less hydrogen would be produced *[1 mark]*. Calcium has a higher molar mass/relative atomic mass/A_r than magnesium *[1 mark]* so there will be fewer moles of calcium available to react than there were of magnesium *[1 mark]*.
   c) Reaction equation:
      $Ba(OH)_2 + 2HCl \rightarrow BaCl_2 + 2H_2O$
      Ratio of $Ba(OH)_2$: HCl = 1:2,
      so moles of $Ba(OH)_2$ required = $0.020 ÷ 2$ = 0.010 mol
      Volume = moles ÷ concentration = $0.01 ÷ 0.65$
      = 0.0153... dm^3 = 15.3... cm^3 = **15 cm^3** (2 s.f.)
      [4 marks for correct answer to 2 s.f., otherwise 1 mark for reaction equation/correct ratio, 1 mark for correct moles of barium hydroxide, 1 mark for correct volume given in dm^3]
   d) Theoretical yield of $MgCl_2$ = $(12.5 ÷ 60) × 100$ = 20.83... g
      Moles of $MgCl_2$ = $20.83... ÷ 95$ = 0.219... mol
      Ratio of $MgCl_2$: $Mg(OH)_2$ = 1:1,
      so moles of $Mg(OH)_2$ = 0.219... mol
      Mass of $Mg(OH)_2$ = $0.219... × 58$ = **12.7 g** (3 s.f.)
      [4 marks for correct answer, otherwise 1 mark for calculation to find theoretical yield of $MgCl_2$, 1 mark for correct theoretical yield of $MgCl_2$, 1 mark for correct moles of $MgCl_2$]

6 a) Calcium/Ca loses electrons to form Ca^{2+} *[1 mark]*
      and oxygen/O_2 gains electrons to form to O^{2-} *[1 mark]*.

answers

b) How to grade your answer:
Level 0: There is no relevant information. *[No marks]*
Level 1: Simple statements are made that demonstrate a limited understanding of the chemistry involved.
[1 to 2 marks]
Level 2: There is a good description of the relevant procedure, however explanations may be limited or incomplete.
[3 to 4 marks]
Level 3: There is a clear and detailed description of the relevant procedure, which is supported by explanations that demonstrate a good understanding of the chemistry involved. *[5 to 6 marks]*

Here are some points your answer may include:
Calcium carbonate is an insoluble salt.
Insoluble salts can be made from precipitation reactions, in which two soluble salts react together.
To make calcium carbonate, a soluble salt containing calcium ions must react with a soluble salt containing carbonate ions.
Calcium sulfate is insoluble, so it is unsuitable.
Magnesium carbonate is insoluble, so it is unsuitable.
Calcium chloride and potassium carbonate are both soluble, so are suitable reactants.
Calcium chloride + potassium carbonate → calcium carbonate + potassium chloride
Make solutions of calcium chloride and potassium carbonate by dissolving them in deionised water.
Deionised water should be used so that there are no other ions present.
Stir or shake the solutions to ensure all the salt has dissolved.
Combine the solutions in a beaker and stir well.
The insoluble calcium carbonate will precipitate out.
Filter the solution using filter paper and a funnel to separate the calcium carbonate from the solution.
Rinse the filter paper with deionised water to make sure all of the soluble potassium chloride has been washed off the solid salt.
Remove the calcium carbonate from the filter paper and leave to dry.

Topic 6 — Groups in the Periodic Table

Pages 42-44 — Groups in the Periodic Table

1 a) Astatine will be a simple molecular substance with covalent bonds *[1 mark]*. It is a Group 7 element / has 7 electrons in its outer shell/energy level *[1 mark]* so will form one covalent bond to give both atoms a full outer shell *[1 mark]*.
b) KAt *[1 mark]*. Potassium forms 1+ ions and astatine forms 1− ions when they react *[1 mark]*.
c) There will be no reaction *[1 mark]*. Astatine is less reactive than chlorine, so cannot displace chlorine from a salt solution *[1 mark]*.
d) The outer shell/energy level of rubidium atoms is far from the nucleus *[1 mark]*. Therefore little energy is required to remove the single electron in rubidium's outer shell/energy level, making it highly reactive *[1 mark]*. The outer shell/energy level of iodine atoms is far from the nucleus *[1 mark]*. Therefore it is difficult to attract the extra electron that iodine needs to fill its outer shell/energy level, making it fairly unreactive *[1 mark]*.
e) How to grade your answer:
Level 0: There is no relevant information. *[No marks]*
Level 1: There is a brief description of the similarities and differences between the reactions of lithium and potassium with water, but no explanation of these observations. *[1 to 2 marks]*
Level 2: There is a detailed comparison of the similarities and differences between the reactions of lithium and potassium with water, and some explanation of the observations. *[3 to 4 marks]*
Level 3: There is a detailed comparison of the similarities and differences between the reactions of lithium and potassium with water, and a full explanation of the observations. *[5 to 6 marks]*

Here are some points your answer may include:
A vigorous reaction would be observed with both metals.
Both metals will float/fizz on the surface of the water, because they are less dense than water.
The reaction between potassium and water would be more vigorous than the reaction between lithium and water.
Both metals produce hydrogen in a reaction with water, so bubbles would be observed.
Both metals also produce a hydroxide (lithium hydroxide and potassium hydroxide).
Both have one electron in the outer electron shell/energy level.
The outer shell/energy level of potassium atoms is further from the nucleus than in lithium, so the outer electron is more easily lost.
So potassium is more reactive and produces bubbles faster.
The reaction with potassium gives out more energy.
The heat generated is enough to melt the potassium and ignite the hydrogen produced.
A lilac flame is observed with potassium.
The reaction with lithium does not produce enough heat energy to melt the metal.

2 a) Any two from: e.g. alkali metals generally have lower melting points than other metals / alkali metals are generally softer than other metals / alkali metals are generally less dense than other metals *[1 mark for each correct comparison]*.
b) As you go down Group 1, the single outer electron gets further away from the nucleus / the atomic radius gets larger *[1 mark]*. This means it is easier for the atom to lose the outer electron *[1 mark]*, so the alkali metals get more reactive as you go down the group *[1 mark]*.

3 a) Any value from −185 °C to −109 °C *[1 mark]*.
The boiling points of Group 0 elements increase down the group. Krypton is between argon and xenon, so its boiling point must be somewhere between their boiling points.
b) Group 0 elements exist as single atoms with weak intermolecular forces *[1 mark]*, so have low boiling points *[1 mark]*.
c) Until 1962, Group 0 elements were considered unreactive due to the full outer electron shell/energy level *[1 mark]*.
The experiments provided new evidence that the existing theory couldn't explain *[1 mark]* therefore the theory was modified to include the new data *[1 mark]*.

4 a) When halogens react, they gain an electron in their outer electron shell *[1 mark]*. The further the outer shell is from the nucleus, the less strongly electrons are attracted *[1 mark]*.
Chlorine atoms are smaller than iodine atoms / have a smaller atomic radius / the outer shell of chlorine is closer to the nucleus than in iodine *[1 mark]*. Therefore chlorine is more reactive than iodine and reacts more quickly *[1 mark]*.
b) A purple vapour will form in the beaker *[1 mark]* as the iodine vaporises as it is heated *[1 mark]*. Purple/grey crystals will form on the lid *[1 mark]* as iodine crystallises/solidifies/deposits on the cooled lid *[1 mark]*.

5 How to grade your answer:
Level 0: There is no relevant information. *[No marks]*
Level 1: There is some description of the reaction between chlorine water and sodium iodide, but little or no reference is made to redox reactions or electron transfer. No or an incorrect prediction is made of what would be observed if chlorine water was added to sodium chloride or sodium bromide. *[1 to 2 marks]*
Level 2: There is a description of the reaction between chlorine water and sodium iodide, with some reference being made to electrons being transferred between the chlorine and the iodide ions. At least one correct prediction is made of what would be observed if chlorine water was added to sodium chloride or sodium bromide. *[3 to 4 marks]*
Level 3: There is a detailed description of the reaction between chlorine water and sodium iodide, including an explanation of the fact that the chlorine is reduced and the iodide ions are oxidised. A completely accurate prediction is made of what would be observed if chlorine water was added to sodium chloride or sodium bromide. *[5 to 6 marks]*

Here are some points your answer may include:
Chlorine is more reactive than iodine, so it displaces iodine from the sodium iodide.
Iodine is dark brown when it is in solution, whereas chlorine water is colourless.
So the solution would go from colourless to brown as the reaction occurs / iodine is produced.
The reaction is classed as a redox reaction because electrons are lost by one reactant and gained by another / a reduction reaction and an oxidation reaction happen simultaneously.
The chlorine is reduced to chloride ions as it gains electrons from the iodide ions.
The iodide ions are oxidised to iodine as they lose electrons to the chlorine.
If you added chlorine water to sodium bromide, the chlorine would displace bromine from the solution, so the solution would go from colourless to orange.
If you added chlorine water to sodium chloride, there would be no reaction as the solution already contains chloride ions / chlorine cannot displace itself from solution. So no colour change would be seen.

Topic 7 — Rates of Reaction and Energy Changes

Page 45-48 — Rates of Reaction

1 a) B *[1 mark]*
The size of the measuring cylinder won't affect the results so long as the correct volume is still measured out.
   b) E.g. with 20 cm³ of $Na_2S_2O_3$ the time taken is 22 s and with 10 cm³ the time taken is 44 s, so doubling volume halves time / doubles the rate of reaction *[1 mark]*. Doubling volume doubles concentration / volume is proportional to concentration *[1 mark]*.
The volume of the $Na_2S_2O_3$ stock solution is proportional to the concentration because the total volume of stock solution and water is kept the same. So if more stock solution is used, less water must be used and the concentration will be higher.
   c) Doubling concentration doubles the number of particles in the same volume *[1 mark]*. This doubles the frequency of (successful) collisions *[1 mark]*.
   d) Increasing the temperature gives particles more energy / makes them move faster *[1 mark]* so the particles collide more often and the rate increases *[1 mark]*. The particles also collide with more energy *[1 mark]* so more of the collisions are successful / have sufficient energy to react / have the activation energy *[1 mark]*.

2 a) Gradient = change in y ÷ change in x
= (102 – 50) ÷ (4.5 – 0) = 11.555... = **12 cm³ min⁻¹**
[3 marks for an answer between 11 cm³ min⁻¹ and 13 cm³ min⁻¹ given to 2 significant figures, otherwise 1 mark for drawing a tangent and 1 mark for using the correct equation to calculate the gradient.]
   b) The gradient of the graph is initially steep, but it starts to decrease / get less steep as time increases *[1 mark]*, so less carbon dioxide is produced in a given amount of time *[1 mark]*.
   c) A *[1 mark]*

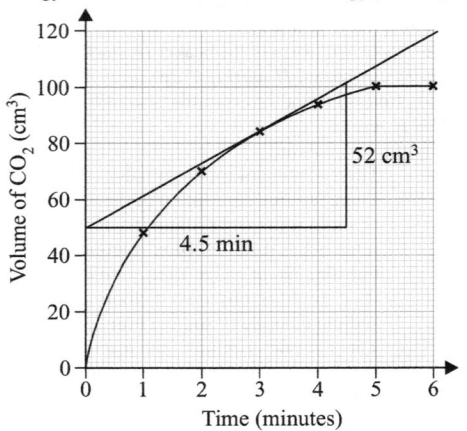

3 a) *[4 marks — 1 mark for a correct calculation of loss in mass (y) values, 1 mark for at least 6 points plotted correctly, 1 mark for correctly labelled axes with sensible scales (taking up more than half of each axis), 1 mark for a line of best fit.]*
   b) Mean rate of reaction = change in y ÷ change in x
= (0.0405 – 0.0315) ÷ (35 – 15) = 0.009 ÷ 20 = **0.00045 g s⁻¹**
[3 marks for answer between 0.0004 and 0.0005, otherwise 1 mark for a change in loss in mass between 0.008 and 0.010 and 1 mark for equation to calculate mean rate of reaction]

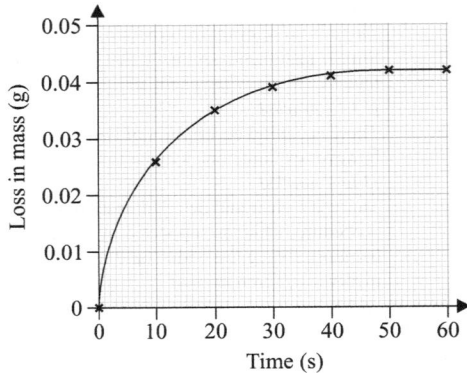

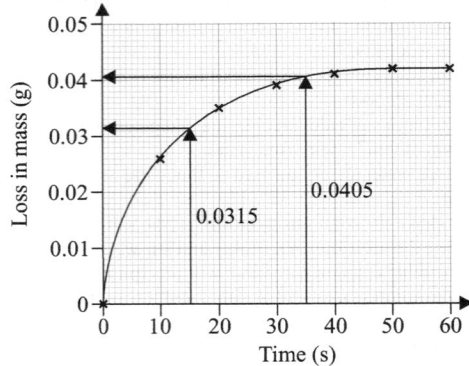

4 a) A greater mass of powdered catalyst provides more surface area for collisions/the reaction to take place on *[1 mark]*.
   b) How to grade your answer:
Level 0: There is no relevant information. *[No marks]*.
Level 1: There is a brief attempt to explain how either the first method or the second method could be used to calculate a rate of reaction. The points made are basic and not linked together. *[1 to 2 marks]*
Level 2: There is some explanation of how both the first and second methods could be used to calculate rates of reaction, but the answer is missing some detail.
It may not be clear how the second method provides more evidence to support the conclusion.
Some points are linked together. *[3 to 4 marks]*
Level 3: There is a clear and detailed comparison of the two methods, as well as a full explanation of how the second method provides more evidence to support the conclusion. The points made are well-linked and the answer has a clear and logical structure. *[5 to 6 marks]*

Here are some points your answer may include:
Recording the volume of gas collected in 60 seconds allows the mean/average rate of reaction to be calculated for each mass.
The average rate can then be compared for each mass.
The results can be plotted on a graph of mass of catalyst (x) against volume of gas (y).
Recording the volume of gas produced at intervals between 0 and 60 seconds, e.g. every 10 seconds, allows the rate of reaction at any point to be calculated.
This can be achieved by plotting a graph of time (x) against volume of gas (y), drawing a tangent to the curve at a particular time and calculating the gradient.
Dividing volume of gas by time taken gives the rate.
The rate at any point during the 60 seconds can be compared for each mass.
This provides more information than average rate of reaction, e.g. it can be used to see if/how the rate varies over the course of the reaction. This can be used as more evidence to support a conclusion.
Very fast reactions may be over before 60 seconds, so just taking a reading at 60 seconds might not give different results.

Answers

c) E.g. filter off the catalyst after the reaction, then wash and dry it *[1 mark]*. Reweigh the catalyst and compare the masses before and after the reaction *[1 mark]*. The catalyst is not used up during the reaction, therefore there should be no change in mass *[1 mark]*.

Pages 49-50 — Energy Changes

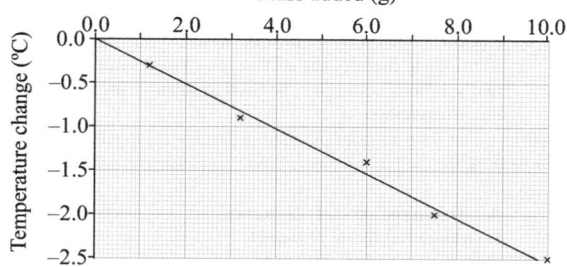

1 a)

[3 marks — 1 mark for axes with a sensible scale (taking up more than half of each axis), 1 mark for all points plotted correctly, 1 mark for a sensible line of best fit]

b) −1.3 °C *[1 mark for any answer in the range 1.2-1.4 °C]*
You get this value by reading off the temperature change for 5 g from your line of best fit.

c) E.g. the student has used a polystyrene cup / placed a lid on the cup *[1 mark]*, which will prevent energy transfer to the solution during the experiment *[1 mark]*.

d) As the reaction is endothermic, the energy released by bond formation must be less than the energy absorbed by bond breaking *[1 mark]*. The reaction must have a low enough activation energy that enough particles have sufficient energy for the reaction to proceed at room temperature *[1 mark]*.

2 Energy released by bonds forming in the products
= 2 × (3 × N–H) = 2 × (3 × 391) = 6 × 391 = 2346 kJ mol⁻¹
Overall energy change = energy required to break bonds − energy released by forming bonds, so
Energy required to break bonds = overall energy change + energy released by forming bonds
= −97 + 2346 = 2249 kJ mol⁻¹
Energy required to break bonds = (1 × N≡N) + (3 × H–H)
= 941 + (3 × H–H) = 2249 kJ mol⁻¹, so
(3 × H–H) = 2249 − 941 = 1308 kJ mol⁻¹
H–H bond energy = 1308 ÷ 3 = **436 kJ mol⁻¹**
[4 marks for correct answer, otherwise 1 mark for correct energy released by forming bonds, 1 mark for correct energy required to break bonds and 1 mark for (3 × H–H)]

Topic 8 — Fuels and Earth Science

Pages 51-52 — Fuels

1 a) Hydrocarbon A = $C_{10}H_{22}$ *[1 mark]*
Hydrocarbon B = C_8H_{18} *[1 mark]*
Hydrocarbon C = C_2H_4 *[1 mark]*

b) How to grade your answer:
Level 0: There is no relevant information. *[No marks]*
Level 1: The relative length of the hydrocarbons is stated, and there is some brief description of properties, but no attempt at comparison is made. No attempt is made to explain the desirability of hydrocarbon A. *[1 to 2 marks]*
Level 2: The relative length of the hydrocarbons is stated, and there is some comparative description of the properties of both hydrocarbons. An attempt is made to explain the desirability of hydrocarbon A. *[3 to 4 marks]*
Level 3: A full, clear comparative description of both hydrocarbons is made, and the desirability of hydrocarbon A is explained. *[5 to 6 marks]*

Here are some points your answer may include:
Both hydrocarbons are alkanes.
Hydrocarbon A is a shorter chain hydrocarbon than $C_{35}H_{72}$.
Hydrocarbon A will be less viscous than $C_{35}H_{72}$.
Hydrocarbon A will be more volatile/have a lower boiling point than $C_{35}H_{72}$.
Hydrocarbon A will be more flammable/easier to ignite than $C_{35}H_{72}$.
Hydrocarbon A is more useful as a fuel than $C_{35}H_{72}$.
Hydrocarbon A/decane is used in fuels such as kerosene.
Demand for hydrocarbon A will be higher than for $C_{35}H_{72}$.

c) $C_{10}H_{22} \rightarrow 3C_2H_4 + C_4H_{10}$ *[1 mark]*

2 $2NO + O_2 \rightarrow 2NO_2$ *[1 mark]*
$2NO_2 + H_2O + 0.5O_2 \rightarrow 2HNO_3$ or,
$4NO_2 + 2H_2O + O_2 \rightarrow 4HNO_3$ *[1 mark]*

3 a) $C_8H_{18} + 12.5O_2 \rightarrow 8CO_2 + 9H_2O$ or,
$2C_8H_{18} + 25O_2 \rightarrow 16CO_2 + 18H_2O$
[1 mark for correct products, 1 mark for correct balancing]

b) E.g. $C_8H_{18} + 9O_2 \rightarrow 2C + 3CO + 3CO_2 + 9H_2O$
[1 mark for correct products, 1 mark for correct balancing]
Your products must include C and H_2O, but CO and CO_2 don't need to be there (or you can just have one of them).

c) The solid particles of carbon that form can worsen respiratory problems *[1 mark]*. Carbon monoxide combines with red blood cells / stops red blood cells carrying oxygen around the body *[1 mark]*. High levels of carbon monoxide can lead to fainting, a coma or death *[1 mark]*.

4 Demand for $C_{16}H_{34}$ is not as high as demand for shorter hydrocarbon molecules *[1 mark]*. Cracking breaks longer alkanes into shorter alkanes and short alkenes *[1 mark]*. Short alkanes are used as fuels (e.g. for cars and aeroplanes) *[1 mark]*. Short alkenes are valuable as feedstock/monomers for producing polymers *[1 mark]*.

Pages 53-55 — Earth and Atmospheric Science

1 a) How to grade your answer:
Level 0: There is no relevant information. *[No marks]*
Level 1: Simple statements are made describing the trend in carbon dioxide levels or suggesting its effect on at least one of the factors. *[1 to 2 marks]*
Level 2: A description of the trend in carbon dioxide levels is given, along with statements that suggest the effect on both factors, or give an explanation of the effect on one factor. *[3 to 4 marks]*
Level 3: A description of the trend in carbon dioxide levels is given and is used to provide full explanations of the suggested effects on both factors. *[5 to 6 marks]*

Here are some points your answer may include:
The level of carbon dioxide in the atmosphere at the South Pole increased between 1960 and 2010.
The rate of increase of carbon dioxide has risen as time has progressed.
CO_2 is a greenhouse gas.
Greenhouse gases accumulate in the upper atmosphere.
Greenhouse gases allow short wavelength radiation from the sun to pass through them to Earth's surface.
Greenhouse gases absorb long wavelength radiation that is reflected off the Earth. They re-radiate this in all directions, including back at the Earth.
This is the greenhouse effect.
Increasing levels of CO_2 enhances the greenhouse effect, causing a rise in global temperatures/global warming.
This increases the global average surface temperature.
Increased global temperatures cause the polar ice caps to melt.
The melting of the polar ice caps causes sea levels to rise.
This increases the global mean sea level.

b) E.g. there are no direct records of carbon dioxide levels from that long ago, so the historical data will be an estimate (based on fossil analysis, tree rings, or gas bubbles trapped in ice) *[1 mark]*. Historical data is often based on measurements taken from fewer locations than modern data, so it's less representative of global carbon dioxide levels *[1 mark]*.

2 a) Earth's early atmosphere had a much lower level of oxygen than the atmosphere today because there were no/fewer plants/algae *[1 mark]*. Plants and algae evolved over time and began to produce oxygen *[1 mark]* through photosynthesis, which increased the levels of oxygen in Earth's atmosphere *[1 mark]*.

b) Venus' atmosphere has a much higher percentage of CO_2 than Earth's atmosphere *[1 mark]*. CO_2 is a greenhouse gas *[1 mark]*, so a higher percentage of CO_2 leads to more warming of the planet and therefore an increased surface temperature *[1 mark]*.

c) E.g. Fossil fuel consumption and carbon dioxide /
Livestock farming and methane.
[2 marks for naming a correct human activity and giving a corresponding gas]

Answers

84

3 How to grade your answer:
Level 0: There is no relevant information. *[No marks]*
Level 1: There is a brief overview of both studies. However, there is no attempt to make a comparison or a conclusion. *[1 to 2 marks]*
Level 2: There is an evaluation of both studies with an attempt at a conclusion. However, some points are missing or lacking in detail. *[3 to 4 marks]*
Level 3: There is a clear evaluation of both studies with a reasoned and well-supported conclusion. *[5 to 6 marks]*

Here are some points your answer may include:
The first study was conducted over a longer period of time than the second study, so there is more data available that supports the conclusion of the first study.
The first study measured the temperature twice per year, whereas the second study measured the temperature annually, so there is more data available that supports the conclusion of the first study.
The first study collected data across the whole country, whereas the second study only collected data in one location, so data for the average annual temperature for the country is more reliable in the first study.
The first study has a greater sample size than the second study, so it is less likely to have been affected by anomalous results.
The first study has been peer-reviewed, which means that the data and method have been checked by other scientists, making this study more reliable.
It is unknown if the second study has been peer-reviewed, which means that it might not have been checked for false claims and it could have been carried out unscientifically.
The conclusion of the first study supports the general scientific consensus about climate change, whereas the conclusion of the second study disagrees with it.
The second study is not inconsistent with the first study, as a rise of 0.5 °C over 50 years averages to 0.1 °C every 10 years.
The second study is more likely to be biased as it has been carried out by an oil company that may want to disprove that greenhouse gases cause climate change in order to continue making money.
The second study is more likely to be biased as the oil company may be less concerned about climate change, as they are based in a part/ the north of the country which is less likely to be at risk from the effects of climate change.
There could be key information missing about both studies if the news report has described the studies in an inaccurate or over-simplified way.
It's not clear from the report how the scientists in the first study arrived at their prediction for the future temperature rises.
From the information given, the first study is more reliable than the second study, so is more useful when considering the effects of climate change on the country.

Topic 9 — Separate Chemistry 2

Pages 56-57 — Tests for Ions

1 How to grade your answer:
Level 0: There is no relevant information. *[No marks]*
Level 1: Simple statements are given suggesting tests for positive and/or negative ions. The answer lacks detail and ideas are not linked or logical. *[1 to 2 marks]*
Level 2: An explanation is given that would allow positive and/or negative ions to be confirmed. Explanations, however, may be incomplete or imprecise and limited in terms of linking ideas / showing logical reasoning. *[3 to 4 marks]*
Level 3: A detailed and accurate answer is given, that would allow both positive and negative ions to be confirmed. Explanation involves linked and sequential ideas and logical reasoning. *[5 to 6 marks]*

A logical series for identification of the ions would be:
Flame test using the loop of nichrome metal. Clean the loop in acid between each test.
The two samples containing sodium give a yellow flame.
The two samples containing potassium give a lilac flame.
Produce a solution of each salt by dissolving a sample in deionised water.
Add nitric acid to solutions of A, B, C and D, and the sample containing the carbonate ions will fizz.

Add silver nitrate to the remaining three samples — a white precipitate will show the presence of chloride ions and a cream precipitate will show the presence of bromide ions.
Take a further (fresh) sample of the remaining solution and add dilute hydrochloric acid followed by barium chloride solution — a white precipitate confirms the presence of sulfate ions.
Alternatively, hydrochloric acid could be added to A, B, C and D first, in which case the carbonate would fizz as above, but barium chloride solution could next be added to the remaining three solutions to identify the sulfate ion. Fresh samples of the remaining two solutions could then be used to identify the halide ions, as described above.

It's important that fresh samples are used to identify the halide ions if using the latter method because they will all contain chloride ions after the addition of hydrochloric acid.

2 a) A Lithium iodide (LiI) *[1 mark]*
B Orange-red flame *[1 mark]*
C White precipitate *[1 mark]*
D No visible change *[1 mark]*
E White precipitate *[1 mark]*

b) $Ca^{2+}_{(aq)} + 2OH^-_{(aq)} \rightarrow Ca(OH)_{2(s)}$
[1 mark for balanced ionic equation, 1 mark for state symbols]

3 a) Element A *[1 mark]*.
None of Element A's spectral lines match those of the sample.

b) Element B has a spectral line at 550 nm and spectral lines below 400 nm *[1 mark]*. The intensity of the spectrum indicates the concentration of an ion, so the sample is likely to contain a higher concentration of element B than of the other elements *[1 mark]*.

Pages 58-59 — Reactions of Organic Compounds

1 a) C *[1 mark]*
There is a carbon atom with 5 bonds.

b)
```
      H   H       H
      |   |       |
  H — C — C = C — C — H
      |       |   |
      H       H   H
```
[1 mark]
E.g. the structure has the same (molecular) formula / it is C_4H_8 / it has the same number of carbon and hydrogen atoms as the structure drawn by the student, and it contains a double bond *[1 mark]*.

c) The alcohol is butanol *[1 mark]* and has the chemical formula C_4H_9OH *[1 mark]*. Butanoic acid has the chemical formula C_3H_7COOH *[1 mark]*.
The chemical formulas are written this way to show the functional groups.

d) The carbon-carbon/C=C double bond breaks *[1 mark]* and a bromine atom is added to each of the carbon atoms *[1 mark]*. Bromine is now part of a new molecule/compound/product which is colourless *[1 mark]*.

2 a) Glycolic acid has the functional groups of both an alcohol, -OH, and a carboxylic acid, -COOH *[1 mark]*.

b) Fizzing is observed *[1 mark]*. The carboxylic acid functional group reacts with sodium carbonate to produce carbon dioxide *[1 mark]*.
$2CH_2OHCOOH_{(s)} + Na_2CO_{3(aq)}$
$\rightarrow 2CH_2OHCOONa_{(aq)} + H_2O_{(l)} + CO_{2(g)}$
[1 mark for correctly balanced equation and 1 mark for correct state symbols]

c)
```
     O      O—H
      \\   /
       C—C
      /   \\
  H—O      O
```
[1 mark for the correct structure]
The alcohol functional group reacts to form a carboxylic acid functional group *[1 mark]*.

Page 60 — Polymers

1 a)
```
      F   F              ⎛ F   F ⎞
      |   |              ⎜ |   | ⎟
  n   C = C      →       ⎜ C — C ⎟
      |   |              ⎜ |   | ⎟
      F   Cl             ⎝ F   Cl⎠ₙ
```
[1 mark for a repeating unit that shows two carbon atoms with a single bond between them and 1 mark for correctly placed n on each side of the equation]

b) Condensation polymerisation *[1 mark]*
The monomers react together and ester links form between them to make a polymer chain *[1 mark]*. A carboxylic acid group reacts with an alcohol group and water is lost for every ester link that forms *[1 mark]*.

Answers

c) How to grade your answer:
Level 0: There is no relevant information. *[No marks]*
Level 1: Simple statements are made about the problems associated with producing and/or disposing of polymers. However the answer lacks detail and no reference is made to the continued use of polymers. *[1 to 2 marks]*
Level 2: Some problems associated with producing and disposing of polymers are given in detail and a simple explanation is given of the continued use of polymers. *[3 to 4 marks]*
Level 3: A detailed and accurate summary of the problems associated with producing and disposing of polymers is given. The properties of polymers are used to explain why polymers are still widely used. *[5 to 6 marks]*

Here are some points your answer may include:
Problems with polymers:
Plastic polymers are made from crude oil, which is a finite resource. As crude oil runs out, plastics and other products made from crude oil will become more expensive.
Lots of plastic waste is generated each year.
Most polymers are non-biodegradable so are not broken down by micro-organisms.
Burning plastic polymers to dispose of them can release toxic gases into the atmosphere. These are harmful to humans/animals/plants.
Burning plastic polymers produces carbon dioxide, which is a greenhouse gas linked with climate change.
Plastic waste fills up landfill sites, which in turn take up valuable land.
Separating polymers for recycling is often difficult and expensive.
If polymers are not separated before recycling, the quality of the final recycled product can be reduced.
It is only possible to recycle polymers a limited number of times as the strength of the polymers decreases over time.
Advantages of polymer use:
Polymers with many different useful properties can be produced by altering the arrangement of the chains.
Many polymers are cheap to produce / flexible but tough / easily mouldable / unreactive / thermally and electrically insulating.
The desirable properties and low cost of plastic polymers means they are still widely used despite the difficulties of producing and disposing of them.

Pages 61-63 — Nanoparticles

1 a) The cube would be classed as a nanoparticle, as it has a side length between 1-100 nm *[1 mark]*.
b) Surface area of cube = 12 × 12 × 6 = 864 nm^2
Volume = 12 × 12 × 12 = 1728 nm^3
Surface area to volume ratio = 864 : 1728 = **1 : 2**
[3 marks for correct answer, otherwise 1 mark for correct surface area and 1 mark for correct volume]
c) Each cube will now have a side length of 6 nm.
Surface area of one cube = 6 × 6 × 6 = 216 nm^2
Total surface area = 8 × 216 = 1728 nm^2
Volume = 1728 nm^3
Surface area to volume ratio = 1728 : 1728 = **1 : 1**
[2 marks for correct answer, otherwise 1 mark for total surface area]
You could also find the surface area to volume ratio of just one of the smaller cubes, as the ratio is the same for one of them as it is for all eight.
d) D *[1 mark]*
As you decrease the side length by a factor of 3, the surface area to volume ratio increases by a factor of 3.
2 a) As the size of the nanoparticle decreases, the total surface area per gram will increase *[1 mark]*, therefore more drug can be bonded per gram of nanoparticle *[1 mark]*.
b) A *[1 mark]*
Area of one side = (100 × 100) = 10 000 nm^2
Surface area = (10 000 × 6) = 60 000 nm^2
Volume = (100 × 100 × 100) = 1 000 000 nm^3
Surface area to volume ratio = 60 000 : 1 000 000 = 3 : 50

c) Surface area of Nanoparticle B = 25 × 25 × 6 = 3750 nm^2
Volume of Nanoparticle B = 25 × 25 × 25 = 15 625 nm^2
Surface area to volume ratio = 3750 : 15 625 = 6 : 25
[2 marks for surface area to volume ratio, otherwise 1 mark for calculating at least one of surface area or volume]
This is four times as great as the ratio for Nanoparticle A *[1 mark]*, so four times as many drug molecules can be attached per unit volume *[1 mark]*.
6 : 25 is equivalent to 12 : 50, and the ratio for Nanoparticle A is 3 : 50, so the ratio for Nanoparticle B is 12 ÷ 3 = 4 times greater.
d) E.g. the particle model assumes particles are identically-sized solid spheres. This may not be true for the nanoparticles *[1 mark]*.
3 a) E.g. silver nanoparticles are able to kill a range of microorganisms, so skin products that contain silver nanoparticles could be used in situations where antimicrobial properties are required *[1 mark]*. Silver nanoparticles are soluble in water, so could be added to water-based products easily *[1 mark]*. Silver nanoparticles are very small and might enter the body through the skin, the risks of which are not well understood *[1 mark]*. Silver nanoparticles can release toxic ions when dissolved, which could be harmful to humans if they end up inside the body *[1 mark]*.
b) i) E.g. for each process, the scientist has treated and analysed three samples of water and taken a mean of the results *[1 mark]*, which will reduce the effect of any random errors in the results *[1 mark]*. / The scientist has taken all of the untreated water samples from the same source *[1 mark]*, which will prevent any differences in the results being due to differences in the untreated water *[1 mark]*.
ii) E.g. the scientist could have repeated the analysis of each individual water sample multiple times *[1 mark]*.

Pages 64-67 — Properties of Materials

1 a) composite *[1 mark]*
b) E.g. low carbon steel is cheaper *[1 mark]*.
c) E.g. aluminium corrodes less than low carbon steel *[1 mark]*.
2 How to grade your answer:
Level 0: There is no relevant information. *[No marks]*
Level 1: Simple statements are made about the advantages and/or disadvantages of the polymers. However, the answer lacks detail and no attempt at a conclusion is made. *[1 to 2 marks]*
Level 2: An evaluation is made based upon the majority of the information provided. However the conclusion reached is not supported by the points included in the answer. *[3 to 4 marks]*
Level 3: There is a clear, logical evaluation of the materials with a reasoned conclusion. *[5 to 6 marks]*

Here are some points your answer may include:
Both polymers are suitable based on being unreactive with water.
Both polymers have similar chain lengths, so that provides no advantage either way.
Polymer A is cheaper than Polymer B.
Polymer A is lighter than Polymer B.
Polymer B won't stretch under force, so it is stronger than A.
Hot water pipes would not be heated to 500 °C, so this characteristic is not relevant.
Hot water pipes may be heated to nearly 100 °C, and so this characteristic is relevant.
Polymer B is more resistant to heat/hot water than Polymer A.
Although it is more expensive, Polymer B is the best material for the piping as it is more heat resistant and stronger than Polymer A.
3 a) 100 − (4.5 + 0.6 + 1.5 + 0.5) = 92.9 % aluminium
(92.9 ÷ 100) × 68 500 = 63 636.5 = **63 600 kg** (to 3 s.f.)
[2 marks for the correct answer, otherwise 1 mark for the correct percentage of aluminium]
b) The student is incorrect. The tensile strength increases with increasing percentage of copper until around 65% *[1 mark]*, but as the percentage of copper increases above 65%, the tensile strength decreases *[1 mark]*.
c) From the graph, pure copper (100% copper) = 22 000 kPa.
8% copper = 18 000 kPa
22 000 − 18 000 = **4 000 kPa** *[2 marks for correct answer, otherwise 1 mark for 22 000 kPa and 18 000 kPa]*

4 a) E.g. heat resistance/cost *[1 mark]*.
   b) How to grade your answer:
      Level 0: There is no relevant information. *[No marks]*
      Level 1: Simple statements are made about the advantages and/or disadvantages of the ceramics. However, the answer lacks detail and no attempt at a conclusion is made. *[1 to 2 marks]*
      Level 2: An evaluation is made based upon the majority of the information provided. However the conclusion reached is not supported by the points included in the answer. *[3 to 4 marks]*
      Level 3: There is a clear, logical evaluation of the ceramics with a reasoned conclusion. *[5 to 6 marks]*
      Here are some points your answer may include:
      Ceramic A is the weakest ceramic in terms of both compressive strength and tensile strength.
      Ceramic A has the lowest value for fracture toughness so would crack more easily than ceramics B and C.
      Ceramic B has the same density as ceramic A, but is considerably stronger and has a higher value for fracture toughness.
      Ceramic C is the strongest ceramic in terms of both compressive strength and tensile strength.
      Ceramic C has the highest value for fracture toughness so would crack the least easily out of the three materials.
      Ceramic C is the densest of the three materials so would make the heaviest plates, which is impractical.
      Ceramic B is the best material to make plates from because it is stronger than ceramic A, but not as dense (and therefore heavy) as ceramic C.
   c) E.g. alumina is inert, which means that it will not undergo any reactions which could potentially damage either the alumina or the body *[1 mark]*. Its strength and relatively high fracture toughness mean that it is unlikely to break under stress *[1 mark]*.

5 a) Metal B is pure copper because it has the lowest tensile strength *[1 mark]*. Pure metals have layers of metal atoms that can slide over each other *[1 mark]*, making the metal malleable and soft, and therefore weaker *[1 mark]*.
   b) i) The data shows that nichrome has a higher tensile strength than pure nickel *[1 mark]*, which suggests the addition of chromium increases tensile strength in this case *[1 mark]*.
      ii) E.g. there are only two data points in the table, so there isn't enough data to see if there's a clear trend between the amount of chromium in nichrome and tensile strength *[1 mark]*. Tensile strength might not increase consistently with chromium content, so more data points are required to establish a correlation between the two *[1 mark]*. / There is no data in the table for any other chromium-containing alloys *[1 mark]*. Chromium alloys containing metals other than nickel might have different properties, so the conclusion cannot be made for all alloys *[1 mark]*.

Mixed Questions for Paper 2

Pages 68-73 — Mixed Questions for Paper 2

1 a) A = bromine *[1 mark]*
     A more reactive halogen displaces a less reactive halogen from an aqueous solution of its salt *[1 mark]*. A reacts with potassium iodide solution to displace iodine, so A must be a halogen that is more reactive than iodine *[1 mark]*. Chlorine reacts with an aqueous solution of A's salt, so A must be less reactive than chlorine *[1 mark]*.
     The only halogen that is more reactive than iodine but less reactive than chlorine is bromine.
   b) Z = potassium *[1 mark]*
      Formation of a white, soluble (ionic) solid with bromine/vigorous reaction with water to form an alkali implies Z is a Group 1 metal *[1 mark]*.
      E.g. the formula for a Group 1 metal hydroxide is ZOH, so the percentage by mass of the OH$^-$ ion = 100 − 69.64 = 30.36%.
      M_r(ZOH) = 17 ÷ 0.3036 = 55.99... *[1 mark]*
      So, A_r(Z) = 55.99 − 17 = 38.99... = 39 *[1 mark]*
      (so Z is potassium)
      You could also use trial and error to work this out. The percentage by mass of Z in ZOH = A_r(Z) ÷ (A_r(Z) + 17) × 100. This must equal 69.64%. If you try a few different alkali metals, you'll only be able to get this value with potassium (A_r = 39) — sodium would give you 57.50%, lithium would give you 29.17%.
   c) E.g. a white precipitate will form *[1 mark]*. Chlorine reacts with aqueous lithium iodide to form iodine and chloride ions in solution *[1 mark]*. The chloride ions react with the silver nitrate to form a white precipitate of silver chloride *[1 mark]*.
   You won't get a yellow precipitate of silver iodide because all the iodide ions will have been displaced from the solution to form iodine, I_2.

2 a) E.g. buckminsterfullerene is a hollow sphere *[1 mark]*, which means it can cage the drug molecules inside *[1 mark]*. It is also very small *[1 mark]* which could help it to be absorbed by the body *[1 mark]*.
   b) E.g. the nanoparticles could get into parts of the body they aren't meant to and damage cells *[1 mark]*.
   c) In carbon nanotubes, each carbon atom is bonded to three others *[1 mark]* with strong covalent bonds *[1 mark]*.
   d) Each carbon atom forms only three covalent bonds, so has one delocalised electron *[1 mark]*. This electron can move through the nanotube and carry an electric charge *[1 mark]*.
   e) Nanotubes have a high surface area to volume ratio *[1 mark]*. Reactions take place on the surface of solid catalysts *[1 mark]* so a large surface area means more collisions and a faster rate of reaction *[1 mark]*.

3 a) E.g. the student could add a lid to the calorimeter, which would reduce energy loss to the surroundings. / the student could use the thermometer to stir the water/clamp the thermometer with the bulb in the centre of the beaker, so that their reading represents the temperature of the all of the water and not just the part directly above the flame.
   [1 mark for any sensible suggestion and 1 mark for explaining how it would improve the accuracy of the result.]
   b) E.g. ethanol/methanol *[1 mark]*. More of alcohol X is required to raise the temperature of the water by 25 °C, so alcohol X is a less efficient fuel than propanol *[1 mark]*. The shorter the carbon chain, the less efficient the fuel *[1 mark]*, so alcohol X must have a shorter carbon chain that propanol *[1 mark]*.
   c) The products are at a lower energy than the reactants *[1 mark]*.
   d) There would be a greater difference in height between the reactants and the products on the reaction profile of pentanol *[1 mark]*. This is because pentanol has a longer carbon chain than propanol, so it is a more efficient fuel *[1 mark]*. Therefore, for the same mass of fuel, pentanol will release more energy *[1 mark]*.
   e) How to grade your answer:
      Level 0: There is no relevant information. *[No marks]*
      Level 1: Simple statements are made about the production of ethanol from the fermentation of a carbohydrate. However, points are not linked and any conditions stated are not explained. *[1 to 2 marks]*
      Level 2: A description of the method for producing ethanol from the fermentation of a carbohydrate is given, and an explanation of the necessary conditions is attempted. Points are linked together, however some points/explanation may be missing or incorrect. *[3 to 4 marks]*
      Level 3: There is a clear, logical description of the method for producing ethanol from the fermentation of a carbohydrate. Necessary conditions are given with clear explanation. *[5 to 6 marks]*
      Here are some points your answer may include:
      Mix some yeast and a solution of a carbohydrate/glucose in a clean container.
      Yeast is used because it contains an enzyme that works as a catalyst/speeds up the conversion of the carbohydrate to ethanol.
      Seal the container and leave it in a warm place.
      Keep the mixture between 30 °C and 40 °C.
      Fermentation happens fastest between these temperatures.
      At lower temperatures, the reaction is slow.
      At higher temperatures, the enzyme becomes denatured/destroyed and the reaction stops.
      The reaction must be carried out in anaerobic conditions/without oxygen present.
      This is because oxygen will convert the ethanol to ethanoic acid.
      When the concentration of ethanol reaches 10-20%, the reaction stops. This is because the ethanol kills the yeast.
      The yeast falls to the bottom of the container.
      The ethanol solution can be collected from the top of the container.
      The ethanol solution can then be distilled to the desired concentration.

Answers

4 a)

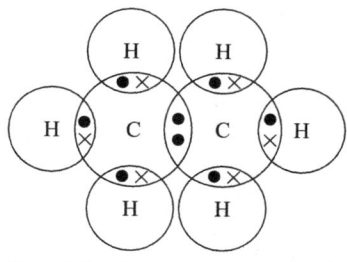

*[1 mark for elements correctly labelled,
1 mark for correct electronic structure]*

b) Carbon has four electrons in its outer shell *[1 mark]*. Each carbon needs four more electrons for a full outer shell *[1 mark]*. Two of these electrons come from forming two single covalent bonds with hydrogen atoms *[1 mark]*. The other two come from sharing two pairs of electrons with the other carbon atom to form a double bond *[1 mark]*.

c) The student is incorrect, because the covalent bonds within simple molecules are not broken when the substance boils *[1 mark]*. Instead, it is the intermolecular forces that are broken *[1 mark]*.

5 a) i) Iron is a pure metal, so it has layers of metal atoms *[1 mark]* that can slide over each other *[1 mark]*. Iron oxide has an ionic lattice structure *[1 mark]*, in which the ions are fixed in position and cannot slide over each other *[1 mark]*.

ii) number of moles = number of ions ÷ Avogadro's constant
moles of Fe^{3+} = $(4.50 \times 10^{24}) \div (6.02 \times 10^{23})$ = 7.4750... mol
number of moles of Fe_2O_3 = 7.4750... ÷ 2 = 3.7375... mol
mass = moles × M_r = 3.7375... × 160
= 598.0066... = **598 g (3 s.f.)**
[3 marks for the correct answer, otherwise 1 mark for calculating the number of moles of Fe^{3+}, 1 mark for calculating the number of moles of Fe_2O_3]

b) i) Addition of aqueous sodium/potassium hydroxide *[1 mark]* will cause a green precipitate to form if iron(II) ions are present *[1 mark]*. The compound is iron(II) hydroxide *[1 mark]*.

ii) $Fe^{2+}_{(aq)} + 2OH^-_{(aq)} \rightarrow Fe(OH)_{2(s)}$
[1 mark for correct reactants and products, 1 mark for balancing, 1 mark for correct state symbols]

c) Manganese/Mn could be present *[1 mark]* because all the lines in the spectrum of the manganese solution (4041, 4783 and 6022) are also present in the spectrum of the metal ion solution *[1 mark]*.

6 a) Sulfur dioxide in the atmosphere mixes with water in clouds to form acid rain *[1 mark]*. Acid rain acidifies lakes, which can kill aquatic species *[1 mark]*.

b) i) Energy required to break the original bonds
= (2 × (S = O)) + (2 × (O − H)) + (0.5 × (O = O))
= (2 × 522) + (2 × 459) + (0.5 × 494)
= 2209 kJ/mol
Energy released by forming bonds
= (2 × (S = O)) + (2 × (O − H)) + (2 × (S − O))
= (2 × 522) + (2 × 459) + (2 × 265)
= 2492 kJ/mol
Overall energy change = 2209 − 2492 = **−283 kJ/mol**
[3 marks for correct answer, otherwise 1 mark for calculating energy used breaking bonds, 1 mark for calculating energy released when bonds are formed]

ii) The energy required to break bonds has decreased by
(0.5 × (O = O)) = (0.5 × 494) = 247 kJ mol⁻¹.
The energy released when bonds are formed has decreased by
(1 × (S = O)) = (1 × 522) = 522 kJ mol⁻¹.
So the overall energy change = −283 − 247 + 522
= −8 kJ mol⁻¹
[3 marks for the correct answer, obtained using answer to part i), otherwise 1 mark for decreases in energy required and energy released, 1 mark for correct calculation to use these values to adjust the answer to part i)]

The Periodic Table

	Group 1	Group 2												Group 3	Group 4	Group 5	Group 6	Group 7	Group 0
Period 1							1 H Hydrogen 1												4 He Helium 2
Period 2	7 Li Lithium 3	9 Be Beryllium 4												11 B Boron 5	12 C Carbon 6	14 N Nitrogen 7	16 O Oxygen 8	19 F Fluorine 9	20 Ne Neon 10
Period 3	23 Na Sodium 11	24 Mg Magnesium 12												27 Al Aluminium 13	28 Si Silicon 14	31 P Phosphorus 15	32 S Sulfur 16	35.5 Cl Chlorine 17	40 Ar Argon 18
Period 4	39 K Potassium 19	40 Ca Calcium 20	45 Sc Scandium 21	48 Ti Titanium 22	51 V Vanadium 23	52 Cr Chromium 24	55 Mn Manganese 25	56 Fe Iron 26	59 Co Cobalt 27	59 Ni Nickel 28	63.5 Cu Copper 29	65 Zn Zinc 30		70 Ga Gallium 31	73 Ge Germanium 32	75 As Arsenic 33	79 Se Selenium 34	80 Br Bromine 35	84 Kr Krypton 36
Period 5	85 Rb Rubidium 37	88 Sr Strontium 38	89 Y Yttrium 39	91 Zr Zirconium 40	93 Nb Niobium 41	96 Mo Molybdenum 42	[98] Tc Technetium 43	101 Ru Ruthenium 44	103 Rh Rhodium 45	106 Pd Palladium 46	108 Ag Silver 47	112 Cd Cadmium 48		115 In Indium 49	119 Sn Tin 50	122 Sb Antimony 51	128 Te Tellurium 52	127 I Iodine 53	131 Xe Xenon 54
Period 6	133 Cs Caesium 55	137 Ba Barium 56	139 La Lanthanum 57	178 Hf Hafnium 72	181 Ta Tantalum 73	184 W Tungsten 74	186 Re Rhenium 75	190 Os Osmium 76	192 Ir Iridium 77	195 Pt Platinum 78	197 Au Gold 79	201 Hg Mercury 80		204 Tl Thallium 81	207 Pb Lead 82	209 Bi Bismuth 83	[209] Po Polonium 84	[210] At Astatine 85	[222] Rn Radon 86
Period 7	[223] Fr Francium 87	[226] Ra Radium 88	[227] Ac Actinium 89	[261] Rf Rutherfordium 104	[262] Db Dubnium 105	[266] Sg Seaborgium 106	[264] Bh Bohrium 107	[277] Hs Hassium 108	[268] Mt Meitnerium 109	[271] Ds Darmstadtium 110	[272] Rg Roentgenium 111								

Relative atomic mass →
Atomic (proton) number →

The lanthanoids (atomic numbers 58-71) and the actinoids (atomic numbers 90-103) are not shown in this table.